T0146902

STOP PRESSURING ME

STOP PRESSURING ME

AMI DZISSAH

Copyright © 2015 by Ami Dzissah.

Library of Congress Control Number:		2015907613
ISBN:	Hardcover	978-1-5035-6910-2
	Softcover	978-1-5035-6909-6
	eBook	978-1-5035-6908-9

All rights reserved. No part of this book may be reproduced or transmitted in any form or by any means, electronic or mechanical, including photocopying, recording, or by any information storage and retrieval system, without permission in writing from the copyright owner.

Print information available on the last page.

Rev. date: 05/27/2015

To order additional copies of this book, contact:
Xlibris
1-888-795-4274
www.Xlibris.com
Orders@Xlibris.com
713180

ENGLISH

If I was born English
And breaded English
I don't know what difference to make
But sure
I will make a dream at young

I love the English
I love the language
I love the style
Still, I am proud to be African.

But if I was born and breaded English
I would use the language well
And would not have a problem
With its vocabulary.
I'll be smart in all my classes
Because, it's all English vocabulary.

If I was born English
I would be no better
But, at the language.

This book attempts to heighten the awareness of bullying behaviors, and for students to learn and cope more effectively.

Introduction

This book is a revised version of my first book, The Westerners; which was published in 2005. The book also consists of collection of poems by the author. The author focuses on bullying behaviors; peer pressures and provides a guide to effective ways of coping. Although the experience of bullying depicted in this book occurred in High school, bullying is everywhere; from the time children start school into adult life comprising of work and relationships. I have experienced it first hand as a high school student, as an adult in my work areas, and I have seen my children also experience it. I find it a duty to heighten the awareness of bullying and peer pressures once again with the hope that young people will learn and cope in a more effective manner. In the book, Selom, a foreign student from Africa tells about her encounter with bullying and peer pressures at first hand. In her ability to cope in an effective manner, she found strength in recognizing her good qualities over the bad qualities of the bullies. She found strength in engaging in activities in and outside of her school, and she engaged in activities that she was passionate about such as writing. Her experience is not only told in a story telling manner, but through some of her collection of poems found at the end of the book. I hope that anyone who has been bullied can relate to this girls' story. Anyone who is being bullied can recognize it as a problem, and lastly be guided to overcome the powers of big bullies. This is based on a true life's story.

CHAPTER ONE

We have just graduated from high school and some us look forward to going on vacations while others think of what to do with their lives in the next six months. In the meantime, we patiently wait for our examination results from the West African Examination Council. To visit a country like the United States of America is the dream for many of my friends. For me, it had been in preparation in the past six months. Although my parents never mentioned it, I knew the moments I was taken to have passport pictures for the first time.

On the plane for the first time away from my friends and family, I was on my way to America. Upon arrival, my dad and I stayed with my aunt in the city of New York. After few days of great site seeing, my father left the U.S, and I continued my education in a Catholic school. I was placed in eighth grade although I had just completed ninth grade in my country. I wasn't happy about that, but it was a foot into the system of America's education. I was sixteen years old. It was already late in September, and the high school didn't accept me because I had low reading scores after taking the American standard Catholic School Entrance Exam. The Junior high School where my aunt taught became a place for me to start. I looked so small and young for my age; no one could have guessed I was sixteen. The students were younger than I, but they looked older and taller. It was embarrassing when they asked of my age, and I would tell them that I was fourteen. I was excellent at the sciences, math and writing. My only problem was reading and understanding when the students spoke. I did not understand the American English language. The teachers were very kind to me. Sometimes I felt dumb because I would say "yes" by nodding, although I didn't understand a thing. At the same time, it seemed fun when I came home, and I thought about everything that happened in school. My good grades and personality made me well known and loved by everyone including the principal. She had asked if she could take me to the movies sometimes along with my classmates on a weekend. It was very kind of her, but I was afraid and could not accept. My aunt was the only black teacher in the school, and she was one of the best teachers, but she was very strict. The kids end up knowing all their alphabets and numbers. They were able to tell shapes and colors, read and write their names. What more could a kindergarten kid learn?

In the winter, I carried my aunt's book bag from school and on the weekend, I did the same and accompanied her to her second job. I would then return home to do grocery shopping and cook for everyone in the house of three. I did Laundry for the two of us and cleaned the house every weekend. It was tiresome and annoying when the wind blew off my scarf; my nose would be running, and I would have a headache. I walked home through the snow before I take some Tylenol. When she returned home, I put her food on the table and waited until she finished. I cleaned up after her and washed the plates before going to bed or finish my school homework. At times, I felt tired from cleaning the house all day, but I had to wait for her to fall asleep before I can take a break. She calls my name a million times to get her socks, pillow, an ear pad or a glass of water while laying on the lazy couch. Lord have mercy on me, I used to pray. Each morning I made her tea with lime before we both left for school. Her forehead was full of thick lines, and that used to scare me because she didn't smile much. The School was where I had fun. We played hide and seek, both boys and girls, and I cannot believe how close and friendly we all were in the school. I would rather be in school all week than go home. I felt like a slave for the first time in my life. And as a well-raised church girl, there was no bone of rebellion in me.

I graduated a year later with the certificate of academic excellence. We took pictures as many as we could, and I will forever remember such people in my life. My Stepmom and my two sisters, Lisa and Lillian, arrived the next day from Ghana, and I was so glad because I missed them a lot. They helped me with the chores around the house, and nothing changed with my aunt except she tried to be kind to my stepmom and my sisters. My stepmom slept on a blanket on the living room floor while my sisters and I shared a full-size bed in the small second bedroom. We later decided to move to our uncle's house, and we left at night into a room where the girls slept on a king-sized bed, and my stepmom had a separate room. Later we rented the basement portion of his house. We shared the basement with an elderly man as a roommate. He got the bedroom, and we got the hall. Luckily there was a door that divided the hall and the bedroom, and we could put a lock on that door. Not long, our stepmom left and had told my uncle to find us public schools to attend. She strongly advised us on how to live, how to protect ourselves, and how to not depend on anybody to do anything for us. "If you do well you do it for yourself, and it's the same when you do badly," that is what she and my dad said all the time. Lisa and Lillian quickly gained admission at my old school, and I went on to St. Barnabas high school before my stepmom left. After the first marking period in the school, I was moved to Regent's classes, and I loved the challenge there. I had friends in every class and was never made fun off nor criticized for who I was and from where I came.

A couple of months later my dad also visited and stayed for about three weeks, and he stayed upstairs with my uncle. With my dad, it was always fun because he took us shopping initially, and he lived us with some allowance.

At about six months after my dad left, my stepmom returned again with my two brothers. She found us public schools where we all continued the rest of our education. I spent my next term as a freshman in Public high school. It would be a new experience for my siblings and I to attend public school. We moved again into our own single bedroom apartment away from family members, and our life was different as we lived on our own. Our parents did not visit as often as they did before because we had four other younger siblings back in Ghana, and we learned to use the strict discipline we have been breaded with, to survive.

CHAPTER TWO

The Public high school was an entirely different world compared to the private schools I had attended. My school was of all kinds of races. People were Caribbean, Africans, Black Americans, Indians, and a few Whites Americans. The first time they noticed me I wore my Catholic school blue skirt and a leotard. I felt all eyes were on me, and I loved the attention for a moment. Good legs Babe! Someone shouted as I walked down the hall. In my classroom, I came across this boy named David. It was like a sudden beam of light, and I took my eyes off immediately. The different hair and clothing styles the other girls wore, made me feel a little different and often nervous whenever I went to school. I felt I did not fit in. My hair was fussy with curly braids. A girl stopped me in the hallway and said, "David likes you."

"I don't like him", I said.

Why? She asked.

"I just don't," I answered.

I had a class with him, and I was glad I did. He sat two desks in front of me. He read well, and I liked him for that. Whenever he turned back, I did the same in order not to see his face. After class, he followed me down to the lunchroom; pointing at me to a boy whose name I did not know. As I got in the lunchroom, the door closed and he remained outside. I felt a strong heartbeat each time I saw him. I had most classes with him, and he showed up in all of them. I loved his attention, but I had put my head down as I walk by him. The girl met me again in the hall and said, "David wants to go out with you."

"I don't think so", I said.

Why? She asked.

I just don't.

There were these other boys in the lunchroom that made fun of me. They said I was ugly, and that made me felt awful to be in the school. There were days that I did not want to return to the same school again. There was one boy who watched me as he let out the words YOU ARE UGLY!. Often when I entered the lunchroom, I did not know what table to sit on because the boys occupied most. I manage to find a table, and as I sat by myself, I felt that many people were staring at me. I put my food aside as if I was done eating and then I took a book to read instead. I couldn't eat because I felt too much attention was on me. I asked myself, what the heck is going on and I wish I had an idea.

In my biology class, everyone seemed kind. They would ask where I came from politely. Ghana, I would answer.

It is in Africa, right?

Yes.

Is it a beautiful place?

"Yes", I would answer.

At the mention of Africa, they could not picture it to be a continent; they could not picture it to have beautiful countries, cities and towns. They could not imagine people wearing clothing, eating, drinking, working and schooling. In their minds, Africa is a huge jungle with people who lived with animals. The teacher began to teach, and so there were no more questions for me to answer. In the locker room, two girls asked me the same questions the other students had asked and when I answered, they laughed, and I couldn't walk with my head up any longer. At home, I could not talk about it because I did not know if my siblings were going through the same thing. Among these people, I thought of what to wear to school the next day every day. The highest price for shoes I wore cost fifteen dollars at Payless Shoe Store. I only had four pants, one tight jean, one baggy and two colored dress pants. I had one long and loose skirt my dad bought me from London, and I loved to wear it with my leotard.

Back in the lunchroom, the boys burst into laughter the moment they saw me in line to get my food. They come to torture me and then go away. I watched who called me 'ugly' because he is the main guy who starts making fun of me, and then the rest of the guys laugh along. His teeth were of different colors, big and small and crooked. He was very skinny, shallow chested and not in the shape of a male. He had no shoulders to attract any girl, and his disproportionate facial features reflect the word cute, only from a distance. They found me weak and mute. Some of them would just stare at my face. They would not say a word; they just stared like they had never seen a human being like me before. One thing I was always afraid of was being asked where I came from. The line in the lunchroom seemed too long, and I was getting tired this time. Others came up to me and said;" You gone stand there like that, girl, they try to 'diss' you, and you gone stand there like that, I would curse them out like shit".

She took the chance to get in front of me, but it was okay with me, and I smiled, because the language sounded very different and funny to my hearing. I had never heard of anything like that in my entire whole life until I came to this school. I left the line and headed downstairs to the library without getting my food. The language kept repeating itself in my head, and I kept on smiling. I never went into that lunchroom again.

I met this senior student, and we got to know each other. I asked if she has ever been tortured in any way since she came to the school. No, she answered, but she explained.

I tell you what girl, you come to school, go to class, do your work and don't bother to talk to them kids who think they all that. They don't know anything, and all they do is to come to school and make fun of others. Are you African? She just asked.

Yes, how do you know that?

I could tell from your accent. I bent my head and smiled.

'When they know you are from Africa, they think it's just a big jungle, I tell you what, "the kids don't read".

At home, I stayed awake all night because I could not sleep. I kept seeing David and just could not get him off my mind. Even when I didn't want to think of him, it just happens. When I fell asleep, I saw him in my dream talking to me, and I did not know what he was saying exactly. When I woke up, I felt terrible about the dream.

At school, I was walking to my English class in the morning when my shoelace loosened up. I tripped and fell in the midst of these students in the hallway. I felt utterly humiliated, and all they said was, "Oh, shit!" then they laughed. How rude they were, these people had no sense of pity for a human being. One of the teachers came out of his classroom and helped me pick up my books, and I finally made it to class. One thing I was glad about was that David and the girl weren't there at that moment. The gossip among the girls in the class was too much to absorb. I could not look at anyone's face but the blackboard. Is this it? I asked myself.

I went to bed right after school while my sisters watched Soap Opera and did their homework at the same time. How was I going to face these students tomorrow? Who do I talk to or look at whose face? I have thoroughly embarrassed myself in front of people I see every day; boys, girls and teachers. All they could say was "oh shit," then they laughed. I cried silently in my sleep as I thought about the incident repeatedly.

The next day, I saw David in the hallway and in my social studies class, and I did not want to look at him. In the class as I put my head up to answer a question, he wouldn't take his eyes off me. He and the girl who told me about him, kept staring at me, and as they smiled I frowned at the thought of how nervous he made me feel. I felt so bad about myself and did not want to talk to him. I couldn't look at him in the eye, but I wished he would pass a word to me.

The next day at school, he passed down a note to me, saying that he likes me. I felt so good but stupid; I didn't know what to say but to pass back the note to him. In the library, I could not focus on what I was reading. I kept repeating the same sentence repeatedly. I put away my notebook and picked up a book about love instead to read.

In the Social Studies class, David was absent, but the girl was there. I waited till she finished writing her work on the blackboard. Then, I went up to her and asked if she could tell David that I like him, but I could not go out with him.

Why? She asked.

"I am not allowed to". I replied.

She just looked at me.

In the Homeroom, there he was. We both stared at the same window without knowing until the girl said so; at that moment I slowly turned away. I knew the surrounding girls were looking at me, so I put my head on the desk.

In the hallway the boy who called me "ugly" screamed and laughed as I passed by, and I could not walk with my head up.

The kids in my Biology class seem to be the nicest group of people. Some of the guys would say something like, 'Simon and Selom sounded alike'. They tried to tease with the idea that this other boy likes me, but I knew it to be a joke, and I often don't know the right response to give.

Do you like him? One girl in the class asked.

"No. I don't." I didn't mean to make him look bad, but my response made them laugh.

"Oh, shit she 'dissed' you," she said to Simon.

"Come on, you know you like him," she said to me.

I only shook my head in response to No.

Okay, what is your number?

I shook my head again.

231., one other boy started and expected me to finish.

I ignored them instead.

Come on Sel, I even like your name, he said.

Thank you.

And your number?

No way.

Yes, way.

"You make me laugh", I said, and they all laughed.

On the following Monday, I wore my favorite leotard top, tight jeans and a new pair of sneakers which I bought for fifteen dollars. I had my hair chemically relaxed and nicely styled with some pins on the sides, and I looked good. The students noticed the different look on me as well as David. There was this other boy named Kenny in one of my classes, he jokes around referring to every girl as his girlfriend.

"You are not my boy" Rita said to him.

"You will not get a man like me," he replied.

Ronald is another boy in the class who enjoys any altercation so long as he is not part of it, and he would support whoever was being defeated. He is annoying, but his laughter can be contagious. Rita barely shows up in class, and when she did, she slept on her desk.

Chapter Three

During our eleven days of Christmas vacation from school, everything seemed dull. All we did was watch television. We had no radio or videotapes and were unable to rent movies or listen to music. I chose to write about anything that I could think of, and sometimes it turns out to be a complete story expressing exactly how I felt about the students who made fun of me. My sisters complained about our living conditions, and we all wished life was a bit different. We turned off the television and went to bed instead, even when the weather is good to go outdoors. We could decide to go window-shopping, but can you always go window-shopping and come home empty handed because there is no money? I don't think so. Sometimes I went to a neighbor friend of ours and asked if she could help me get a job. She calls her friends to ask for job openings from their work places and some of them worked in restaurants. I thought of getting a summer job so I could make some money and make my parents not worry about our food and clothing. We could also buy a VCR, a radio, cassettes, and videotapes, and everything will be fine. I went to the supermarket in search of work, and they asked for working papers. I showed them a small green paper from my school, but it did no help. As I went to more stores to pick up application forms, I was often told to try again the next month.

There are many guys in my neighborhood. Some try to stop me each time I pass. If he looked good, I stopped and listened to what he has to say. Kevin would not stop chasing me until a car nearly hit me. I finally gave in and told him all he wanted to know. I couldn't give him my telephone number, and I couldn't go on dates, but sometimes we spent time at the park. He had no problem with that because he worked six days a week. He was twenty-one and a right age for me. He had a car and was a construction worker. He attended night school so he could get his GED. On Sundays, I tell my sisters I was going to church. Instead, meet him at the park. He asked me if I have ever had sex.

How could you ask a question like that? I responded.

"It's just a matter of saying yes or no," he replied.

"It feels stupid to answer to a question like that," I said to him.

Why don't you prove it to me then? He said.

"You must be crazy," I replied.

"You still haven't answered my question", he said.

What if I don't want to answer?

Do you choose to prove it ever to me?

No.

You are afraid!

No. I am not.

Then say something! I can't believe he was laughing throughout this.

Prove it or say it.

You have some nerve.

So, what is it?

Oh no!

It is clear we have no direct parental supervision to guide us through these part of the 'growing up' world, but I'm from a home where parents disown their children for bringing back unplanned pregnancies. All parental support will discontinue including any support for education; worst of all one must marry the big or little man who impregnated her. Not only do I have that fear, but also I have dreams I want to accomplish.

My dad had called that day, and his main concern is if we are we in good health. He asked if we needed anything? No. I replied. In reality, we did, but we want shoes and clothes bought from America not bought from back home. If we said yes, he would bring us already worn boots and shoes, print pants and dresses. I have enough going on in that school just being who I am, how I look, how I sound when I speak, what I wear and saying I am African.

CHAPTER FOUR

It had been a long break from school, and David is in most of my classes. In one class, he moved from one seat to the next until he sat closer, but the teacher told him to get back to his seat. In my Biology class, the teacher talked about the different blood types, and he said that some of them were found mostly among Africans. To make it clearer, he said, "It is believed that it came from individual animals in Africa." At the mention of Africa, there was silence in the room, and I began to feel somewhat uncomfortable. Faces started turning from one end to another, and I had the feeling that something wrong was about to happen. Simon put up his hand and asked if the teacher was talking about all parts of Africa. The teacher did not get to answer the question before Ronald rose up his hand. Without the teacher's permission to speak, he asked, do you mean Africans like Selom? The class burst into laughter except for the teacher, Simon and a few other students. What is funny? One of them asked in an effort to quiet the class. He asked, what is the difference between black people and Africans anyway? He went on to say that Africa was the first place of human existence if they didn't know. "You people are stupid, you fucking blood clot," he said to them. The teacher managed to get everyone to be quiet. All this time, my hand was under my chin and my elbow on top of my desk. My eyes focused on my book; I could not look up to see the board. Selom, Rita called, and I ignored her. "He just 'dissed' you, and you sat there like that", she said. The teacher continued to teach; not realizing how much I was hurt. I felt my blood pressure rising, my heart beating fast and tears began to fill my eyes. I tried not to cry, but the tears flew down my cheeks. Since the teacher dictated while writing on the board, I listened and wrote everything. Even when he was just explaining, I kept on writing because

I did not want to look up and see any one's face. I could not help myself any longer, and the tears flew down my cheeks as much as they could. Fortunately, it was almost time to the end of the class, and no one had noticed me crying until I got up, and Simon told the teacher that I was crying. As I headed down the stairs, I heard someone say, "You, what you did isn't fair at all". "It was just a question", I heard from Ronald's voice of guilt. When I got to the gym's locker room, I proceeded to the bathroom to gather my emotions in order to get ready for Gym class. At the Gym class, we sat on the floor listening to the teacher talk about sex and the need for protection. Then, my Biology class teacher showed up and asked to speak me. I went to the door and listened to him as he talked. "I will call Ronald's parents tonight", he said. He apologized for what had happened, and I went back to class. I could not eat for the rest of the day, and after doing my homework at home I went to bed right away. The next day, Ronald was on the early bus to school, and I wondered why because I never saw him take the bus before. Outside the school, he stood opposite me, and I could see the expression on his face saying sorry and probably, he had been told to apologize. In the class, Simon asked me for a quarter, and I gave it. Ronald asked for a pencil, and he accepted mine. "Thanks," he said, "you are welcome", I replied. Simon turned and smiled. "Pay back the twenty-five cent tomorrow", I said. What? He asked. "Just kidding", I replied. I did not give Ronald the pencil to be friendly with him, but to make him feel sorry.

In our Global studies class, we had a substitute teacher. He was an old, tall man and no one listened to him. Some of the students stood on the desk making unreasonable noise while others played card games. Some made fun of others but not me this time. Some of the girls were smoking in the corner while others were throwing papers. The civilized ones sat quietly but were not reading. Today Paul, a cute looking guy in the school had decided to join my class and not go to his class. He threw a paper at me, and I threw it back at him. He came forward and asked me why I did that. "Because you hit me with it first," I said to him. He stared at me, and I stared until my eyes seem pleadingly sorry. Then he slowly turned away, and I felt shy and silly. At the end of that class session, I walked to the lunchroom with Taisha and from the table where we sat, the boy who called me "ugly" pointed at me while he was talking to his friend. I began to feel nervous, and I wondered what he must been saying about me. After he had left, Taisha called his friend and asked for what he had said about me. "She has cute eyes", he said. I was speechless, and knew it was the boy's way of saying that he liked me. The other boy could not say that. This friend of his and Taisha are both in my Spanish class, most of the time I allowed him to copy from my work. He looks good, but he probably likes me because he copies my work to earn good grades for that class.

CHAPTER FIVE

In computer class, a student asked me why I carried all of my books to school? Aren't they heavy?

Why do you ask? Will you help me carry them? I replied, and he smiled.

At the gym, we were doing 'hill and toe, hill and toe, slash, slash, slash' kind of dance. Four girls laughed at me, and I did not care because I loved the dance.

It was time for Regents exam, and David sat right next to me. I wore a cotton print African made skirt and a T-shirt, and I had no idea there was a piece of gum on my seat. I finished my exam long before most students, but I was afraid to get up. David might see my buttocks stuck to the gum, so I waited until everyone was out except the teacher. I pulled out my shirt and covered my behind with it then finally walked out of the building. It was the end of the school year; the weather was hot, and my stepmom was back. We were given twenty dollars each to go shopping, and I picked up one pair of jeans and a cheap shirt from Conway store. At nighttime, we went behind the apartment building, and we untied the trash bags, and collected clothes that were thrown away at the end of the winter and spring season. We found jeans pants, shirts, sweaters, and shoes. We brought them home, and we all tried them. Whichever does not fit, we put them back in the trash. After we had selected the good fitting ones, we washed them and then replaced them with our old stuff. None of us liked to do this, but we needed clothes, and so we did, and no one knew about it but us.

When I slept at night, I dreamed of David. This time, I wore a dance costume, and I saw him in tights with his bare chest. He held me at my waist, but I was shy. I woke up early before everyone, and I went through the trash bags behind other buildings in the neighborhood. I found books and large record CDs, I found books on 'The Romantics and The Victorians', and a book of poetry as well. Never did we ever think of picking up the pieces someday in our lives. Back home we were rich but over here we're poor. Back home, we lived in our own constructed two family detached home. One unit contained no less than five bedrooms. We lived in a large compound with a paved ground. I had a driver who drove me to school and picked me up from school. We had a private tutor after school for Math and English, and another one for French five times a week. We attended the best private schools where our former presidents also attended, and here we are, living a life we never dreamed. If we had heard of a life like this in America, I don't think any of us would ever want to come.

In another dream about David, we sat under a tree, studying until my dad picked me up, and my dad seemed to like him. I didn't understand the meaning of the dream. But I wished David were closer each time the thoughts flashed through my mind. I missed him; I do think I'm in love.

We were back in school, and I have two honor classes, two Regents classes, Foreign Language and Media. I was assigned to have lunch in the freshmen house but. Immediately I realized the boy who calls me ugly was with my classmates during my lunch period, I changed to a different lunch period, and sometimes I went to the library instead. I came across David on my way to the Library, and that strange thing happened again. It is the feeling of a sharp knife that ran through me the first time I saw him. In my regents' classes, no one made fun of me. The only old classmate in the class was Simon, and I always tapped him on his shoulder each time I saw him.

At home, we all had duties to perform. Isaac, the youngest of all was responsible for taking out the trash in the house, Quincy was responsible for cleaning the bathroom, and the girls were responsible for cooking and cleaning. Quincy and Lisa, the youngest sister, seemed to argue all the time because she can't keep her legs and to herself. She always kicked or hit Quincy. Poor Quincy only runs his mouth and never would hit a fly. My stepmom has been with us for three months, and she thought of returning to see the others too. I raised the topic of increasing our weekly allowance to five dollars at least, and she agreed. Looking on my father's side of the story, it just won't happen. I understand they're not working here, changing large amounts of Ghana Cedis into American dollars requires much money to maintain our rent, utility bills, food, and allowance. The truth is we need money sometimes to provide personal items for ourselves. I need money to braid my hair; I want a leather jacket and boots, not these cheap sneakers I have from trash. I am eighteen; I have no job and still looking for one. As an illegal immigrant, no one would offer me any job. Isaac complained that he had been laughed at when he went to school; I faced the same problem I said. His watch, they said was cheap, he's from Africa, and that makes it worse. The kids at the Public schools we attended were so horrible, and I didn't know why. I never talked back or fought them back when they laughed at me because my culture had restricted my tendencies to react to situations in such manner. In my culture, a child is not encouraged to talk back, and from the way I was raised, I had always been too kind to fight anyone or show retaliation in any form. We did not express ourselves as Americans do and so many times I cried because my feelings were hurt. I have never encountered this kind of bad behaviors from any students until now. Initially, it was a shock, and I was too weak to react.

My dad called us to ask how we are doing again. Quincy complains about his schoolwork, and Isaac complains about the cold weather. "My people," my dad said, "please take time, have patience okay. America is the land of opportunity, and the plain ticket from Africa to America is not cheap. You must make the best of it while you can, keep praying to God, and you'll make it okay, please". These were the words he said, and it is true. America is the land of opportunities, and it was up to us to make the best of it.

It was the end of the first marking period, and we all did well bringing home excellent grades.

CHAPTER SIX

Once upon a cold, windy afternoon, I was doing my Spanish class work when I felt a warm palm on my shoulder. It was Tim, "could you help me with my work Sel", he asked.

What don't you understand?

I need some explanations on to how to do this.

I can't explain.

"I need you to," he said.

Okay then.

He had the features of an athlete, tall and broad chested. He's a Jamaican with a short barbered haircut. He faced me directly from where he sat and had his bag under his arm. I felt his attention but tried to ignore it. He'll probably be the first guy I would want to go out with, and that's only if he ever asks, I thought. "Thanks," he said afterward, and then he left. Ever since I've always wanted to talk to him but I didn't know what to say. Whenever our eyes met, we gave each other that shy silly smile. At times, we said hi to each other, and that's it. One time I felt guilty when he did not pass his midterm exam. The teacher had said earlier that if she mentioned your name, you failed, but if she pointed at you to get your paper, it meant you passed. He came forward and stretched his arm for his paper after she called his name. From the look on the teacher's face, I couldn't look at him. I wanted to talk to him immediately after class, but what exactly could I have said? I put my books in my bag then slowly walked out of the class.

Lucy lived a block away from me, so we usually took the bus home together. Well, I told her what had happened, and she advised to talk to him, and also ask if I can help in any way. I wish I could, but I don't know how to start such a conversation with him. I made up my mind that if I went to school the very next day, I would do just as she said, but I just couldn't. After school, I waited in the hall for Lucy, as I wanted to show her who Tim was. We stood opposite the door from which he came, and pretended we were waiting for someone else from that class. As he walked by, we watched his back.

"He is fine," Lucy said.

He plays basketball, number 64

Do you know him?

Of course, I do know him.

We watched him till he was out of sight.

On the following day, a meeting was held in one of the classrooms. We peeped through, and he was in there. We went in and asked about the meeting. It was a Christian club, and they had just begun. They introduced us, and everything else went well. When it was over Lucy and Anthony stood at the back of the class, and they talked for a while. I waited in front so we could go home together. For a while, they were laughing, and I began to wonder what they might have been saying. Finally, we left, and I asked her to tell me why they talked for so long. "About the club," she said, but I knew something was wrong. The next day, he sat behind me in class, so I turned and said hi. He expected me to talk some more, but what was I supposed to say? So you are African. Yes, I nodded.

How old are you? 18.

What grade are you in?

Tenth. What about you? I asked

I'm a junior, and 17. Do you speak Spanish? He asked.

No, I don't.

How come you know so much?

"Huh, I don't know, well I studied French for years, and it's somewhat similar to Spanish. So I find Spanish a bit easier," I said.

Hmm.

The bell rang, and we got up and packed our books. I waited for him so that we could walk out together, but at the door was Lucy, she said hi and then hugged him. Another girl from the other side of the hall also hugged him. Lucy turned and looked at me, and I smiled. When we got to the front of the stairs, he had to go up, and I was closer to him, so I turned and hugged him and then said bye. On the bus, we met Mina. She's from my country too, also a member of the Seekers Club (also known as the Christian club). Lucy sat beside her, and they began to whisper into each other's ears. I felt bad about it but decided to keep my mouth shut. "Sel," I turned to them as Lucy called my name. We know something you don't know, she said. I raised my shoulders in respond. I hated a statement like that, and I didn't talk until we got off the bus.

Why are you so mad? She asked.

I'm not mad.

So how come you're saying nothing, I raised my shoulders again.

Come on Sel, this is not you.

"Perhaps you don't know that much about me than I do," I finally responded.

I don't understand.

You said you knew something about me that I don't, and I want to know.

"It's nothing, come on," she started to laugh. I can't believe you! She said, and I remained quiet. We were close to my building, and I didn't say bye, and left. The next day, I saw Mina, and she asked why I was not talking to Lucy. Because I have nothing to say, I said. She smiled and shook her head. You shouldn't do that, she said. I left, and she followed.

Is it because of what happened yesterday? She asked.

Yes, it is.

It's no big deal!

Why don't you tell me then?

Listen, I promised I wouldn't tell.

"Why don't you accept the consequences of keeping your secret," I replied?

In the school's hallway was Tanya, Hi Sel, Hi, I responded. She looked different, I heard her say to another girl. They have teased and laughed at me, they have called me ugly, and I've kept my mouth shut. Now I have a new hairstyle, shoes with high block hill and some clean pieces from the trash. I have been through sleepless nights and cried. I never threw my arms in any violent act, and even though I've felt that they hated me, I also wished to be like them. I have put on makeup, fake nails, and eyelashes, mini skirt, and bra-like shirt. Now I look entirely different because I look just like them and have friends like them.

CHAPTER SEVEN

At the Christian club today, we began with prayer, praises, then the service. We talked about individuals and woman's virtue. The boys went to a separate room, and a male teacher led them while a female teacher led us, the girls. God created heaven and earth and everything in it, and he saw that they were good. Some people can be beautiful at the sight and gruesome inside. There were a lot more to say, but time was running, and we had to continue at another time. The boys came out, and we closed with a prayer.

On our way home while on the bus, there was a boy who kept staring at me, and then he raised his eyebrow. I moved closer to where Lucy and Mina were sitting, and Lucy finally told me what they said about me.

"Anthony doesn't like you," she said.

How do you know? I asked.

"He told me," she said.

What did you tell him about me?

Nothing.

"He couldn't just come to you and say that he doesn't like me, you might have said something", I said.

Okay, imagine taking a walk in my shoe, can you break a promise you made? She asked.

"Lucy, if you knew you couldn't keep it, you should not have made it. If I do not have to know about it, you should not have told me that you know something I don't know," I responded.

Do you want to know about it? She asked.

I am listening.

I did not want to hurt your feelings, which is why I didn't tell you.

You prefer to talk to Mina about it and make me feel bad.

No Sel, I just can't say it okay.

That's just how long I have nothing to say to you.

Okay, you want to know?

Yes,

I told him how you liked him.

How do you think I like him?

That he'll be the first boy, you'll go out with ever.

Lucy, what made you think I meant that when I said it? I don't even go out, and you know that.

I'm sorry.

Then what did he say?

He only wants you as a friend.

I thought whatever we said between us remained just the between us two.

"I'm sorry, forgive me", she said.

I turned away and said nothing until we got down from the bus. "I'm sorry Sel", she repeated.

Look, I don't know what to say okay, I'll have to think about it.

It's good she stopped by her house because I didn't want her to follow me to my building anymore. Nothing like that had ever happened to me. While doing my homework at home, I couldn't concentrate because I kept seeing him behind me, working with him and handsome is his middle name. How am I supposed to face him in school again? Will I see him and pretend I didn't, to avoid saying hi to him. How could they have done this? I don't know if I can forgive the two of them, I feel betrayed, and heartbroken.

CHAPTER EIGHT

As I was on the bus to school the next morning, I saw Mina run to catch the bus, and she missed it. The driver could still have opened the door because the green light just turned on. She hit the door repeatedly, but the driver refused to open the door. I sat in the back and enjoyed my ride. Surprisingly, she reached school before I did. I was walking with a classmate of mine and ended up standing beside Mina. Hi, she said. Hi, I replied. Entering the building she hadn't her identification card, and I didn't wait for her like I normally would. In class, Tim was early as he usually does on Fridays. He said "hi" and then smiled. Why wouldn't I expect us to work together? He asked. I didn't even turn to look at him. The bell rang for dismissal, and I had my stuff packed already. "Good-bye Tim," I said, and then I left. I knew he expected a hug, but those days are over for me.

It was Thanksgiving Day at the club, and every person had to be thankful for something. It ran from the President of the club, then down to whom ever. I thanked God for everything, my parents and friends. Lucy thanked God for having Mina as a friend; Tim said a lot and so did Mina. In the end, Lucy and I walked to the bus stop together without saying a word. When we got off, it felt so stupid that we walked in the same direction and not talked to each other. She then said something; I didn't hear her clearly, but I laughed as if I heard her say something funny.

Why are you laughing? She asked.

I could ask you the same question too you know.

Does that mean you forgive me?

No.

Do you really mean that?
No, and we both smiled.

Back in school, the students in freshman are fooling in the hallway while classes are in session, and the sophomores are now serious about their classes. Even Paul who used to have braids now have a cute barbered hair, and he leaves for school early because I always saw him at the bus stop in the morning. I didn't see David anymore; probably he's attending all of his classes.

Sometimes, when I thought about my life, I felt I was a parent and a big sister to my siblings, and the expectations of me by my parents are too much. It was my responsibility that everything we needed was in place, and everyone behaved, as they should. As a student, it was very hard for. I had goals of becoming a singer, a writer, and an actor. When I was in class, I felt distracted by flashes of movie scenes in my head, story lines and poems that I felt the need to write down. I went to ask one of the music teachers in the school if he could allow me to join the school's choir. They taught music every seventh period, but I had another class then, and I could not cut a core class for Music. After school would have been better for me, but there was no music lessons held after school.

On the weekend, I went to the library just to keep myself busy instead of staying home. During the previous night, my younger brother left the light and Television on in the living room. If I hadn't gotten up at night to use the bathroom, we would have run electricity current for the whole twenty-four hour period. My second brother did the same thing the very next day, and this made me upset. I removed the plugs and for the whole day, no one watched television but listened to a radio that I recently bought for twenty-one dollars. That was the best punishment I gave them for not shutting off the lights and television before going to sleep. I didn't care about living without a television because I did not watch it as frequently as we do now. My dad never allowed us to watch television although we had one in our home in Africa. We could receive phone calls but were not allowed to make outgoing calls. The bills were supposed to go down and not up, and I had to make sure of that. Living with this two-dollar weekly allowance and these close aged siblings is sometimes unbearable. For the girls, their guts were stronger than mine, and the boys, they just didn't listen.

It was back in Spanish class and I asked the teacher what is good to give a grand mom for Christmas.

"A sweatshirt or a dress will be fine," she replied.

"A kiss" was Tim's idea.

The more I tried to avoid him, the more he tried to get my attention. I had on tight denim and a long sleeve top. My figure vividly showed, and I liked it. Usually, they stared at the front and back of the buttocks, moreover the breast if they're huge. Tim wanted to touch me as he sat at behind me. As he sat down he rested his hands on to my shoulders, "you have wide shoulders," he said, and he squeezed them, and I held his hands. It was embarrassing because the teacher was teaching, and I knew that almost everyone was looking at us. "You have wider shoulders than I do," I replied.

"That's because I'm a man," he said.

"Take your hands off", I said and pinched him softly.

"I'm giving you a massage", he replied.

Finally, the class was over, and I knew he expected me to wait but then another girl drew his attention. So I walked slowly out of the room without saying bye.

In my media class, Joseph liked Rebecca very much. He is a junior and a black American and she is a Jamaican, and a sophomore. Rebecca didn't like him because he acted stupid most of the time. He asked if I found him attractive.

"You are good looking," I said

Do you find me attractive? He repeated.

Attracted to me? No, I replied.

The rest of the guys at the table and those sitting close to us all laughed.

I didn't mean it like that, but his mouth was still opened without a single word out. "All right," I continued, "on a scale of one to ten, you are an attractive looking guy at four." Everyone including Rebecca laughed again.

He turned to her and asked the same question.

"Five out of ten", she said.

He leaned against his seat and shook his head.

Sarah walked in and she turned to me.

So where do you come from? She asked.

I told you before, why do you still ask?

Because I forgot, oh you're African right?

Like I said, I said I told you before.

She expected everyone to laugh, but not single one laughed at all.

So what part of Africa do you come from? She continued

How strangely do I look, and how different do I sound?

"You have an accent," she replied.

I know that, what else?

I'm Jamaican, and you're African.

"She sounds so stupid," I heard Joseph say and the rest of the students laughed.

I wanted to say something awful to her. "Do not talk like you're uneducated," I managed to let out.

Oh, shit! They all said and laughed again, and along the bell did ring. I was infuriated but somewhat; the class reaction was just perfect.

CHAPTER NINE

At school, the girls wore tight jeans with shirts that showed their stomach, and they also wore make-up. I started to dress like them but didn't show my stomach because I didn't feel comfortable with that idea. I realized even Simon whom I thought was a bit decent stared at me like he had never done before. Some boys looked like they would touch the buttocks of the girls, and other boys just stare. It's two things the boys liked, you either have a well-shaped buttock that perfectly fitted in the Jeans pant, or you have big breasts. When I asked Simon for last night's homework, not once did he look up at my face, and I guessed he still looked at my buttocks when I turned away. He sat behind me and stared at my waist. Finally, the bell rang, and he did touch my waist. "Stop it", I said and he only looked at me. I turned away and headed quickly to the library. I saw a girl on a single table, and I walked to her. When I turned, one of the guys had his eyes fixed in my direction. I got up to look for a book about dreams because I want to figure out what some of my dreams about David meant. Instead, I found a book on 'boyfriends and girl-friends'. It didn't say much that interested me, but I looked through it. Anytime I looked up, I saw this boy staring at me, and I found it annoying. I left the book and dashed through the hall just after the bell rang, and then there was David. He just came out of his music class. I didn't take my eyes off him this time, but he did. Oh my God! It was like I won something this time; I did! I was often the shy one who took my eyes off. I was always the one who put her head down because I was ashamed, but I feel a big change. I have some level of confidence, a higher self-esteem than ever, and it felt so good.

There was a dream about a Valentine's Day card on a Christmas night. The card had a big red heart on the front, and blue ink drops on it that read; "I hated him," but I loved him more than I have ever loved myself. What I felt for him is not something I could control, and I never dreamed so much about anyone in my life. The card got me scared when I woke up. I felt like he wanted to talk to me, but he never talked to me. I felt guilty, and as I imagined him, I wanted to throw my arms around him. I wanted to find out what horoscope he belonged to, from Rebecca, but again I'm afraid of what she would think. There was no sign that he was in school that day, and I just wanted to meet him in the hallway as usual.

In Spanish class again, Tim asks to lift me up in front of the class as he does to the other girls, but I refused, because I didn't want to be embarrassed. He went in front of the blackboard and lifted up another girl. She is beautiful, not so tall, and slim and kisses the cheek of almost every guy in the school. He raised her so high that everyone screamed, even the teacher had gotten up from her seat. He put her down then came to me. He started off rubbing my shoulders again, then my earrings and said he liked them. Thanks, I said, then he started moving his hands to my cheeks, down to my neck, then on my shoulders again. I felt he was almost moving his fingers to the top of my breast. I figured he liked me, but he told Lucy that he wanted me as a close friend.

A friend can be of anyone.
He can be a friend of too many girls.
A close friend, he said.
What more could one want than just one to call a friend?
The first time, he talks to a girl in such a tone that will soak her up.
He touches her, making it look like a romantic scene from a movie.
Everyone begins to stare and gossip spread so fast.
What a foolish boy.
He has it all, and the girls fall so quickly
When they ask, you are just a friend, is his response.
Why does he do that?
Maybe it's just who he is, a player!

The Spanish class teacher gave out homemade candies before we left for the Christmas break. A hug and a Christmas wish were what Tim gave me, and simply, so did I. It was a hug he shared with his many close girlfriends before going home.

CHAPTER TEN

I thought I'd plan my days according to this twelve days vacation we had from school. Instead, I had to make up for four days and two weekends because my dad showed up surprisingly on the same weekend we vacated from school.

Day One

I went to Manhattan with my dad to meet some of his business partners. I had no time to go to the library, and we were back at night.

Day Two

I didn't go to church, and no one did. The kitchen was my dwelling place all day long while the rest watched television. I thought I could do something before going to bed, but with the television on 'Seventh Heaven show' I just couldn't help myself.

Day Three

My dad and the boys went out after taking breakfast. I took my book bag and was the first to get to the library. Kids of about sixth to eighth graders later showed up at the door too with the grown ups in college. After two hours of reading definitions and doing model problems. I could no longer concentrate, so I went home. "You are to take Isaac to the clinic because he is not well" Lillian told me, and I left immediately after taking in some butterscotch pudding.

Day Four

My dad, my oldest brother and I walked to Montefiore Hospital to see a specialist because my dad had a stomach ulcer. We learned that my dad had to go to a clinic then get transferred from there if he needed to go to the hospital. In my country, you can walk into any hospital or clinic and ask to be treated. So long as you have money to pay for the care and treatment, no one will deny you medical care. When we got outside, it was snowing and freezing. In a big trashcan, dumped these old and large CD records. They contained excellent songs when I took a good look at them. It was a lot, and I wished I could take all home, but I could only collect a bag full. My dad laughed and said, what will you use these things for, my girl? "I'll play them", I said. Do you have the machine for it? He asked. "I'll buy it". He laughed again. He also searched for a metal, such as brass. He found something that looked like two birds flying and made of copper, and he took them. We took the bus home, cleaned the birds and hang them up on the wall.

Day five

Early morning my dad went out with the boys, and I had a chance to go to the library again. They went for car auction and came back late. At night, we were watching a movie, 'The Breakthrough' and we wanted to see the conclusion when our dad called us to shut the TV off and go to bed.

Day six.

Dad went to the hospital alone, that morning he didn't take breakfast because he said he was going to have surgery. Isaac and Quincy went to the library, Lillian went to the laundry, and I was left home with Lisa. It was so quiet, and that's what I wanted. I studied math and biology and even had time to write some songs and poems before they were all back again. In the evening time, our dad called us from New Jersey, saying he's on his way home. Three hours passed, and we worried because he was not home. There was no one to call to ask about him; he's on the train all by himself at night. He was finally back and didn't seem happy. From our up bringing, we were disciplined in a way that we did not to ask much questions and simply went with the flow.

The day we returned to school after such a short vacation, I made him breakfast so that when he woke up, he will not leave the house without food. I wished I had stayed home with him that day.

In Media class, Joseph sat beside me and asked if I like him again, "no", I said. Another girl passes by, and he asked if he can get some of that 'shit' from the girl.

"I don't know what you're talking about," the girl replied.

"Forget it then", he said, and the guys laughed.

Just how stupid could he be some times?

You, what the fuck is wrong with the number? He turned and asked me.

What number? I said.

Your phone number man, what the fuck is wrong with you?

Do you have a pen and paper? I asked politely, and he grabbed one.

718, Seven, sevens.

Are you sure this is your number?

"If you don't get me on that, just add one", I continued.

"Fuck", he said so loud and the guys laughed. He looked into my eyes and there was no attraction between us. I rose my brows and then blinked.

Do you have a boyfriend? I thought he gave up, but I was wrong.

"No", I replied.

Why?

Why do you ask? I don't want one.

Because you're young and should keep it that way, are you not sixteen?

I nodded in respond to yes because he spoke too loud, and I don't want everyone to know my real age.

"You should be eighteen before you get a boyfriend, I wish my sister hasn't, she's only fourteen", he said.

Everyone laughed; I say he just made my day.

CHAPTER ELEVEN

We ere home after school. Just after watching an episode of General Hospital Soap Opera show, the doorbell rang. It was our dad, we all knew because he's the only one who had not returned. He brought home a big old and dirty teddy bear. "Go to the corner of the building, there were a big couch and a microwave", he said to Quincy and Isaac. He turned, and I had my book bag at my back.

Are you going somewhere? He asked.

"Yes, to the library", I replied.

"Lillian, you go with them," he instructed. Lisa wasn't back during that time, so she was lucky not to be sent out there too to pick up the pieces in broad day light.

I got up and hurried to the first floor. Lillian hates picking up the pieces from the street. Besides it was in broad daylight, and when they came out, I laughed at the expression on her face. I was also lucky at that moment. We do it at night or early morning on weekends when people are still sleeping. That's how we do it when our stepmom was with us. People will stare at them and even laugh. Lillian will not volunteer to do anything like that for any amount of money. When I was back, the couch was inside, and the old one we had in the apartment was taken out. The one from the street looked nicer and bigger than the old one we had. There were more items outside such as, exercising machine, cassettes and more CD records.

"I'll take the exercise machine," said Lisa. I had no choice but to join them pick up the stuffs.

There was a big television too and I wished we could take everything. Isaac found videotapes, and I tried to load my carton with all the CD records.

"Those CDs are out modeled," said Lillian.

"You don't even have the machine to play them," Lisa added.

I got upset because music is a part of me, and anything bad that is said about it was wounding my skin.

"The machine is not sold in stores any longer," Lillian continued.

"Liar," I said.

Girls stop, Isaac suggested.

My two brothers took the TV home, and we later left with the carton of CDs, a box of cassettes and some books. We even found a square clock that looked like a music award with a picture of the Beetles. It worked when Lisa and dad checked it. It was late and we finished our homework at the table while dad went to bed.

Quincy, dad and I walked to the bank the next morning. I hated walking with them because I always walked faster to catch up, and while I feel stupid about it, they laughed. He showed us how to deposit and withdraw money from the bank through the ATM. He had to leave that afternoon, so I went to get my stepmom her favorite candy, that's Nips. He and Quincy went to a different store to buy him some new shirts, and then we all met afterward and returned home. Does anyone have something to say? He asked. "Well, people worry me with this church going stuff, if I tell them I don't go to church then they ask unnecessary questions", Isaac let out. Well, he said, "you don't necessary have to go to church. You go to church when you have the time. I used to love going to church very much but for a while I just stopped. I felt I was giving too much time away. Another thing is, churches today are not very real. They give out envelopes, so you put money in and write your name and amount you give. The more you give, the well known and influential you become in the church. Like I said, they are not real, so I go when I have the time, and you can do the same". He sure made us all laugh. "Listen", he continued, "going to church is unnecessary. You can pray to God, sing to him in your bedroom, and not everyone has to know what you do or whom you believe in. Let's say you have exams in exactly three days. Will you go to an all-night church service for God to help you, or you will study and pray every night so you pass? Especially if you are not as intelligent as some people are, if you go to an all-night church service and you failed, where is your forward going? Hey, I'm not saying don't go to church, but God knows what you do and what you don't do. He knows what you make time for and what you don't.

He has given you the brain and everything else but how to use the brain wisely". He looked up, "hey it is time for me to go". He got up and so did we to help carry the bags downstairs. "So my children take care of yourselves". Before he entered the cab, he gave each of us a handshake, starting from Quincy.

"You are forgetting one thing," I said.

What is that?

Some tip.

Aaah, do you need that?

Yes, everyone said so sharply.

Okay, he reached his hand into his pocket and let out a fifty-dollar bill.

"Ten each", he said.

"But I'm the oldest, and deserve more," I said

"No," the rest disagreed.

"Then, take fifteen and divide the rest among them," was dad's final instruction.

"No, that's not fair," one brother said.

"Oh get away", dad said in a joking manner, and he got into the cab.

Are all these your kids? The driver asked.

"Yes, the first five", was his reply.

You're good! The driver took off, and we all waved goodbye.

That day everything was back to normal. By night, the sink was full of dirty plates, and no one owned up to take care of them, so I did. Isaac threw balls on the couch and wouldn't stop even when Lillian yelled at him. Quincy and Lisa were also faught over sitting on one end of the couch. Lillian and I just sat in the back and watched them do as they pleased.

Quincy had his leg stretched on the couch and wouldn't take them off so she could sit. That's the exact place she wants to sit and would not give up.

"Hey get up," said Quincy.

Will you take your feet off? She asked him.

I say you get up.

If you don't take those feet off, I'm not getting up!

What the fuck do you think you're doing man! He took off his belt and threatened to hit her.

Don't even think of hitting me with that! She yelled

Then get up! He yelled back.

I already told you, if you won't take off your feet I will not get up!

Oh sit, don't get up. He was more calm and relaxed. Isaac has asked of what's wrong with them.

Who? Lillian asks.

He stretched his neck in their direction and said, "them." We laughed.

Listen, I began. You all know better, and I will sit here and watch you fight for as long as you want.

Just a reminder, Lillian added. Keep the tone of your voice down, because there are neighbors in the building.

The next day, Lisa, Isaac and I went shoe shopping with our money from dad. Lisa is tall, so she always picks up a flat hill shoe. She saw this high hill long boot, which drew my attention right away. "I wish to get that but the hills are too long," she said,

"Looks like my type," I said. There were different colors, but I picked something off black. It was the week of tax-free, and it cost me only fifteen dollars to get them.

When I wore the boot to school, it's like I picked the eyes of almost every student.

How much did you buy those? Many asked.

With Taisha, I asked her to take a guess.

Seventy-five dollars?

"Fifteen," I said.

You are kidding!

No, I shook my head.

Where?

On Fordham Road.

For real?

Yes.

Where on Fordham?

From the Payless Shoe Store.

"The boots are cute," and she looked again.

Thank you.

I walked downstairs, and two others yelled out loud.

"I like the boots".

In the hallway, "hey, look at that,"

I hear some say, "wow."

Your boots look cute!

Thank you!

Attention now is more than I ever expected. There is complement wherever I go, and I just loved it.

I did not have enough time to study for the Social Studies and English final exams. For Social Studies, I knew I have failed just after I took the multiple-choice portion. I have been busy studying Biology because I have a lot to study. Our names were called for our test papers and a lot seem jubilant about their grades. With those around me, seeing them jump up and down, yelling at their grades and talking about it got me nervous. I didn't study at all. The teacher called my name and before I got to my seat everyone wanted to know what I got. I shook my head in refusal to show anyone my grade. Simon came up begging, but I was too ashamed. I shook my head many times but still he wouldn't stop asking. Mina also came up, "I can't tell you," I said to her. I felt so sorry I went up to the teacher and asked if the grade will show on the report card. "No," she said and I walked back to my seat. I screwed up, having a fourteen times two out of fifty is no joke. The essay part is worth 25%, and I scored that. In total I still failed. I went up to her again and ask if I can go to the library since we're doing nothing, and she allowed. In the hall, tears run down my cheeks, it was more than a sore on my skin. It was like a wound in my heart. The fact that it wouldn't appear on my report card sounded good, but I still cried because I hate to fail. I heard feet steps and thinking it might be a teacher, I wiped off the tears immediately, but it turned out to be no one. I heard another set of feet steps again and this time, and I hoped it's not my former social studies teacher. He put me in that honors class, and that's exactly where I ought to be. If I saw him, I will feel very much ashamed. I feel like I have disappointed him. No, I don't want to see him, at least not now. I thought of going to cry in the bathroom but what if there were girls smoking in there? I went to the library instead, but didn't feel like staying. I wanted to get out, but I didn't want to go back to that class. As I tried to focus on reading, I saw myself on a big stage again with many people. Should I write down the words of the songs or what? But, I have to study for math; I'm getting too much attention, in the school and I have not been studying much. I could not decide whether to read a book, a magazine or to read my horoscope for the month. I held my head so tight; I don't have to let my conscience control me, and I'm trying not to. I have a math final exam tomorrow, and I have to study. It's not my favorite subject, so I try to do my best. I've got to control myself. Finally I took out the study sheet for math and worked on it. At least that will take my mind off all the other crazy thoughts flowing through in my mind.

CHAPTER TWELVE

An argument arose between a teacher and a student about her grade. Her voice was loud, and She insulted him until a security guard was called to take her out of the class. I didn't understand how they're able to stand up to the teachers like that. In my country, the teacher would beat her up, her parents will whip her more when she got home, and then she will not return to the school for treating a teacher that way.

At home, we talked about our final exams. Quincy scored fifty-out-of fifty on his social studies; I failed, but I did well in Spanish. Lillian had the highest grade in her business class. Everyone else seemed jubilant about his or her grades. I failed one of my favorite subjects, and I feel sorry about that. I feel like I have failed everything. Science was difficult; "I didn't do well," Quincy said.

"For that, I passed," said Isaac.

"Bro, science is hard, and I hate the subject," said Quincy.

"Yea right when you fail, you hate the subject," I said.

"That's true," Isaac said and then laughed.

"No, biology is more difficult and boring to sit and listen to, and I'm tired of seeing that textbook.

Everyone laughed, and then back at the table we all sat to do our homework.

Back in school my Media class teacher gave out our project, and I had an A+, it's a ten-page movie script and I was good at that. You, can I see that? Andrew asked, and I showed him my work.

You did all this?

I nodded.

Did you type all this by yourself?

Chapter Thirteen

We watched General Hospital when Lillian asked if I saw the fight at the school. All I know is there were two girls involved. Quincy, Lisa, and Isaac also returned from school. "Isaac, lock the door", Lisa said, but he didn't. He took off his shoes, hang his jacket, put down his bag and went to the kitchen. There was food in the refrigerator, and all he had to do was to warm it up. Instead, he frowned his face, refused to talk to anyone, then, returned to the living room and turned on the computer and said, "I want to use the computer", and then, he turned the Television off.

I went up to him, and I turned off the computer.

"But I told you I want to use the computer," he said, and I ignored him.

"I'm sorry," he said, and then he turned both the television and computer back on.

Before I went to bed that night, I made sure the windows and the kitchen doors are locked. dishhes were in the sink; no one cared to wash the dishes and I went to bed too. In the morning, my sisters left for school while I was dressing up, and I wore my long boots again. Heading to the bus stop I met Lucy and I thought I was the one late for school.

"You're not late; it's only 7:20," she said.

I often leave at 7:00.

Where did you get those boots?

On Fordham for fifteen dollars.

What, you're kidding!

I can't afford anything more than that.

"You're looking cute in the skirt too," she commented.

Thanks.

In the front of my Math class, two guys were fighting each other's throat. A Hispanic and a black American. They had scratches on their faces with blood, but they won't stop fighting. Security guards were always at the scene to break the fight, but sometimes it's hard trying to separate the two. Down the hall, "you're looking cute" one boy who used to laugh at me in the lunchroom, said.

"Thanks", I replied.

What's your name?

Hmm, interesting, so they didn't even know my name and they used to laugh at me, I wondered.

Why do you ask?

I like you, that's why.

I paused for a while.

We could go out or something, he continued.

You do not understand how much I have disliked the sight of you.

What do you mean?

You used to make fun of me when we were in ninth grade.

What are you talking about?

You need to live me alone.

I left while he looked at my behind. I ran into David when he was about to get into his music class. Our eyes clashed, and it's like a flash of light. I noticed he was about to smile, but I looked away. When I looked back, he was still watching, and I turned away smiling. The chemistry I feel for him is as strong and tight as strings. He is confident and free and just made for me.

The boy I met down the hall showed up in the library and came at my table.

I was hoping we could talk a little more, he said.

About what?

Our freshman year.

Don't you have a class?

Don't worry about that.

Oh, I'm not at all.

Okay, you said I made fun of you, I know my friend did, but I didn't.

You laughed when he did, and it's hard to tell the difference between who was making the jokes, and who was laughing at the jokes.

You are a nicer person than I thought; I'm sorry.

Well, Apology accepted, but I find it abnormal to be friends with someone who made my feelings hurt in a very bad way, I said to him, and then I walked away.

He brought back memories I want to bury, but I know I must be strong and try as much to keep my head up.

CHAPTER FOURTEEN

It is the weekend, Lillian is taking care of the plates in the sink, and everyone else is awake except Isaac. Lisa yells at him to wake up but he did not. She hits him hard with a pillow, and all he said was, "leave me alone." Lisa insisted that he got up. For what ma? Quincy yelled out from the bathroom.

And what do you think you are trying to do? I yelled back at Quincy.

"Oh, my fault."

They sleep in the living room, and they act like it's a private bedroom. later, Lillian and I went grocery shopping. At the supermarket we don't buy milk and eggs. It's either milk or eggs. Lillian insisted on buying eggs instead of milk. I said milk instead of eggs. "Don't do that," she begged, but the milk lasts longer than the eggs. The eggs last for only two days, and the milk lasts for at least a week.

"Four days," she tried to correct me.

It is still better than two days.

Why don't we buy both and keep one for the next week?

You know that won't work. If they see both, they eat them all. We went to the cashier and paid for what we had. At home, we all sat in the living room, and everyone who passed by changed the channel of the television. They left it on an old episode of Hercules and Lisa recites the introduction very well. I wasn't interested in watching, so I went to our bedroom and took my notebook to write something.

The next day we were back in school, and I wished to see David so terribly. I was not ready to talk to him, but I just wanted to see him. He was probably not in school, so my mood was sad. The night before

I had prayed to God, that I want no more attention from the guys. I just do not want anyone to laugh at me so I can be free and be myself.

David spent the time in my Media class the next day. He sat in the front of the class but he turned to face me. I always sat in the back of the class and I tried to focus on watching the movie. It was a movie on basketball, and I am not interested. The teacher put it on because it was nearing the end of the semester, and no one cared anymore. I pretended watching the movie only to get a glimpse of his beautiful eyes and his smile. As he also kept looking at me, I couldn't help it anymore so I pretended to look at the time on my wrist. When I lifted my head, my eyes fell into his, and then the bell rang. I slowly turned, took my jacket from the back of the seat and walked out as I was close to the door.

It had occurred that we would be moving to New Jersey in a few months. Our dad had bought a house there for us to move into. What am I my going to do about David, I wondered. I imagined seeing him when I laid in bed. I had no more dreams about him in a while, and I missed that. Why did I feel so connected to him? The way I felt about him was very strong. What if my parents dislike him when we finally get together? Hmm, that would be another story. Now in the school, I have guy friends everywhere I went. They're cute, good looking, tall and tough. I had picked up a pair of Nike sneakers from the trash, along with my long boots that helped to boost my self-esteem. On the night of the school's award ceremony, the principal said I was beautiful when I went to receive my award on the stage. I felt very good about myself. It was like I was empowered and suddenly renewed, and It felt good. Lillian was among the freshman called for an award too. When I sat among the students waiting and hoping to hear my name, I feared what will happen when my name is called to get an award. Would they clap for me or say something for everyone to laugh at me once again? But at the mention of my name, the crowd made me felt well liked, and I'll miss them all after I leave. I also hoped to make new and wonderful friends in New Jersey. In a short time maybe a boyfriend, too. If I'm lucky some day, David and I will meet again.

At home, I sat in the kitchen, feeling sick with body pains, headache and symptoms of fever. I made myself some tea and put in some ice cubes, that's how I made my ice tea. I went to the living room, and it seemed like Quincy and Lisa couldn't stay in the same place because she wouldn't keep her hands off Quincy. They started with their little argument, and she hit him but not too hard. What was that for? he asked and She laughed. He kicked her and she did not mind him. She then asked for the pillow on the couch that Quincy laid his head on, but he refused. Give me that pillow! she insisted.

For what?

"Give me the pillow I said." She then hit him harder than she had done.

What the fuck is wrong with you? He threatened to hit her back but then she got up and laughed. Then, she sat back down again.

What's the shouting for? Damn! Said Lillian.

Ask him! She pointed at Quincy.

"Don't make me hit you." He threatened to beat her again, but she screamed and got up.

Sel, you have to talk to him! She sat down again in the same spot.

"Don't make me hit you." She got up and sat back down again.

Get up! She said to him.

No! he replied.

Get up I said!

Not this time boy!

"Fine, sit." He got up and moved to the other couch.

Fine! She yelled back.

I went to get Jelly from the refrigerator hoping to feel better after I eat it, but I became rather worse. We had all kinds of pills; Tylenol, Ibuprofen, Vitamins, Theraflu and many others. Our stepmom used to be a nurse, so we knew what to take for simple illnesses. When the sickness got worse, then we went to the nearby clinic. I couldn't finish the jelly, so I handed it to Isaac when he walked into the kitchen.

"Thanks," he said.

Are you okay?

I'm sick.

"Can I get money for bread?" Thinking I would say yes.

"No", was my reply.

Why?

"We spent five dollars on bread alone this week." was my response.

"But I wasn't home", he said.

I was, and I barely got a slice.

He shook his head and walked away. I was feeling dizzy, and the pain got worse. I got up to join them in the living room and asked Isaac to get me my blanket. What's wrong with you? Lisa asked.

"She's sick," Isaac said.

"Get some Tylenol," she suggested, the pills are too big. "When you take them, they get stuck in your throat and don't get down no matter how many cups of water you drink," I said, but they laughed.

Quincy opened the window, and I asked him to close it because I felt too cold.

You're sick.

I know.

He closed it.

I wrapped myself so tight in a blanket and told them to open the window because they were feeling too hot. I finally took some pills and then went to sleep. In the morning, I felt much better. I made tea with lemon and put ice cubes in it to decrease the temperature. I took the pills again, and a few moments later I couldn't wait for butterscotch. A strong bad smell circulated the room. Quincy took his hand to his nose and looked around.

Did anyone do it? he asked.

Isaac laughed.

"It's him," Lisa said.

Quincy kept on laughing.

"It's not me," he said.

Lillian turned to look at me, and then Quincy mentioned my name.

"In case you have forgotten you're sitting close to the bathroom and someone just came out, we all know it was Isaac."

What is closest to your nose? Lisa asked him because he kept looking around. "you cannot take the bad breath of your own mouth." Everybody laughed except him. Lillian looked at me again and said, "It could be Sel".

Had I known the quilt has holes? I replied.

Lisa, Isaac and I laughed. Quincy looked at me and shook his head.

Does anyone want soda from the store? Isaac asked.

I wanted orange.

"Me too," Lillian said.

"I want Coke," said Quincy.

"I want Coke," said Lisa.

"Buy me punch," Quincy changed his mind.

She looked at him and then smiled. "You don't want the same flavor as your worst nightmare," she said, andlaughed.

"You two have a problem," I said.

"I'm saying," Lillian added.

Isaac laughed and shook his head as he walked out of the door to make the purchase of the drinks.

CHAPTER FIFTEEN

I Thought I was done with biology this semester. I studied so hard for it and because of that I failed my math and global studies final exams. After I walked out of the exam room, I had the feeling I have passed; I answered the questions as best as I could. Today is report card day. I scored 50% for global studies, 49% for biology and I passed the rest of the classes with 80s. One thing that took my worry away is the English score. I had an 82 when I thought I was getting a score of 60 or 65. I had June to make up for the biology exam; meanwhile I have Regents exams for Global studies and Math. In ninth grade, I passed all my exams, what happened this time? I promised myself to do much better next semester. I feel sorry when I get bad grades because I care. Many of the students don't care about their grades. Some of them are called super seniors because they don't graduate within the four-year period. The good thing for me is that my parents do not see my grades, but sharing my report card with my siblings made me feel a little good about myself because we all screwed up this time. I don't feel like the oldest and dumbest of this party of five. We're all trying to do out our best.

I have cared so much about my look, what to wear the next day for school, and how to fix my hair and the entire make up I learned to put on. I have dreams about my future, and should not let all that distract me. I used to get nineties and up for Spanish, but this time I made an eighty. It's not so bad as others may see it, but when you know who you are and what you are capable of, you will know when the feeling just isn't right. I have always told myself I want to be an average students, but I didn't know that I was better than that. That was in Catholic school where everyone competed for the best grades, but here its like they don't care. They pick on the few students who study hard and do their best, and I don't understand why.

If we all have the same face,
And have the same height and weight,
There will be no differences.
And no one would make fun of anyone.

I had a couple of days to get ready for June exams. I put away my stories, poems, and songs, and did everything to control all the distractions.

Back to school in September, I had new teachers in all my classes, and I like my social studies teacher very much. He reminded me of my English teacher in 9th grade. I could recollect everything we learned throughout the week without reading my notes or the textbook because he taught that well. The only problem was in English class; we read poems and stories from the book, and the students who read out loud knew what is the story or poem was taught us. The rest of the class either had their heads down on the desk, have their hands under their chin or they stared in the book. They knew when it was the right time to turn over the next page, but remained clueless about the content.

So what do you think of the story? The teacher asked. One girl who does not pay attention, raises her hand.

"It's all right", she said.

The story was good, but those who weren't reading or paying attention say it's boring.

What's the theme of the story? The teacher asked gain.

Another student gave an answer, but she was wrong.

Another student gave another wrong answer.

"That's good", the teacher said in order no to offend anyone. "Who else have something to say about the theme of the story?" The teacher asked again.

The class is boring, one other student said, and she was right.

A fight broke outside the school between two girls. A lot of students surrounded and watched as they faught and cursed each other. I saw Lucy heading to the bus stop, so I run to catch up with her. On the bus, she talked about her so-called boyfriend.

You know what?

What?

I have a valentine.

And who is that if not Charles.

Lesley.

What?

Charles was never my boyfriend.

Not to my knowledge.

Hell no! Charles was just a friend.

He must have been a very close friend indeed.

Stop.

Lucy, you used to dream every night about him.

It was just a dream

Every night?

Okay, we broke up.

Since when?

A long time ago.

Like I'm supposed to believe that. You used to talk about him like he was 'Mr. Best'.

She laughed and then explained.

Listen, we haven't talked for a long time, his friend came and told me that he's going out with another girl okay, so I figured we broke up.

What did you do?

Nothing, what do you expect?

Something like, go to him and ask why he did that. Why do you have to find out from his friend?

He'll just be like, I'm sorry, and I don't want to hear that.

I think you still like him.

No.

He's right across the street from your house.

I know.

Hmm, why don't you tell me about this other guy?

Well, it's one of his friends.

We got off the bus and continued.

"Don't do that," I said.

Do what?

It's one of his friends.

Sel, its the first time a guy asked if I could be his valentine, it sounded so sweet when he said it, and I said yes, what do you think?

What I think is you should not hang around any of his friends.

She laughed, and then said, will you be my valentine? She repeated the words to herself.

At home, we were about to watch the Fresh Prince of Bell Air and Lisa sings the introductory song so well.

Will you shut the fuck up? Quincy yelled at her, but she ignored him.

"Damn it", He said.

Isaac stood beside me. "There's no food in the house", he said and I ignored him.

There's no food Sel,

What do you mean?

You go to the kitchen and see for yourself.

There's dry smoked fish and rice, and if you cannot cook, too bad for you. What do you do when we cook? I asked him.

You only know how to eat, Lisa added. I mean you two, she pointed at both boys.

You don't even help clean the dishes, you don't want to do any work around the home, but eat a lot, I said. "The laziest people", Lillian added.

They said, we should make use of what is available, dry smoked fish from sweet home Africa, and rice. They don't give us money to buy chicken or beef. Even clothes we need to wear, they brought homemade dresses and pants, and then you go to school and everyone laughed at you because you look different. For me to have good sneakers, they brought a pair from back home, and it wasn't new. That sneakers caused me to fall in the middle of the school's hallway, and all the kids said was, oh shit!.

"Well you can get your two dollar allowance and go to the Chinese place around the corner if you want to", Lisa suggested.

That two-dollars is not given out at the beginning of each week; I said, and all the girls burst into laughter.

At school, Tamika and I sat at the same table in the study hall. The boy who called me "ugly" showed up suddenly, and he was alone, so I felt at ease. He talked to Tamika and he kept turning and looking at me.

I didn't say a word, and I turned away when he came nearer. Tamika had a gift from a boy, so Shawn wanted to find out who gave her the gift.

So do you love him? He asked, and she ignored.

Her small bottle of sunny delight was on the table, and he grabbed it.

Can I drink some? He asked

"Sure," she said.

I could not share a bottle of anything with anyone. He put the remaining half down.

"You could drink all if you want to," she suggested.

You sure you don't want it? He asked. I was glad she didn't take back that bottle.

So what are you doing here? She asked.

Nothing.

Don't you have a class or something?

I have Gym class.

Hmm.

Why don't you go then?

I forgot to bring my gym clothes.

That happens every day, I thought.

I have heard of a playwriting, essay and poetry contest. Teachers read some of my work and they seemed to like it. One said she will know about me some day, and I pray for that day. If I could not get a job, perhaps competing in the writing contests is the best thing to do with the hope I may win some cash. I may not be legal to work but writing is free and opened to everyone. At night, I wrote in my journal in the kitchen while everyone was asleep.

Back in class we had a substitute. Others were playing cards, talking or sitting like Sheila and I. I thought she called my name, so I turned. "Sit in front of me so we can talk, "she said.

Do you have a boyfriend? She started.

"No", I replied.

In what grade are you?

Tenth.

How old are you?

Sixteen, but I'll be seventeen in April".

"I'll be seventeen in May.

Do you have a boyfriend? I asked

"Yes, we've been going out for seven months"

What do you do when you go out?

You've never been out?

No.

For real, I don't believe you.

Why?

Do you come from Africa? She asked.

"Yes", I replied.

For real, what is it like? I want to go there, is it a beautiful place?

Yes, there are big houses, hotels, everything you need.

So you never had a boyfriend, never been out, wait let me get a pen, what's your phone number?

I can't tell you.

Why?

I'm not allowed to.

Do you listen to your parents?

Not everything they say.

Do you work?

No.

Me neither.

The bell rang.

Where do you come from? I asked.

Trinidad.

I thought you were a Jamaican.

She shook her head in response to 'no'.

"I'll see you tomorrow", she said.

I nodded and said bye. Walking down the stairs, I hit a boy with my book bag in the hallway. He was in a hurry, and I was trying to get through the crowd.

Ouch! he said, and I stopped and turned. I knew I didn't hit him that hard.

You hit my testicles! He said.

I opened my mouth in shock. "That isn't true", I said.

Do you called me a liar?

I hit your stomach.

So what do you say?

I'm sorry.

The crowd laughed; I shook my head and then smiled and left.

I'm back to my old self again except I had my hair in braids. No more make-ups, and I didn't worry about my look anymore. I felt okay with almost everyone in all my classes. The problem I continued to have is with the students who made fun of others. Most of the time, they were the group of girls and boys who stood in the hallway, and they talked about everyone. It is worst when you have classes with them. They criticized what someone is wearing, and they often thought they were better than everyone. Regardless of their size, they wore tight shirts and pants. Their hair was as short as mine, and they changed wigs every week. I thought I look better than they did, but I didn't know why they always laughed at me. Today they laughed hard when I passed by, I decided not to turn, but then they mentioned my name so loud, I turned and saw their fingers pointing at me. My head was down once again and I hurried through the crowd. I felt my heart beating faster while on the stairs; I felt like crying, but I didn't want to. I went to the library and tried to focus, but I couldn't because I kept hearing them call my name. I wanted to know what it is with me, is it my hair, what I'm wearing, or is it just me? I see nothing wrong with me! There's nothing or anyone like the word 'perfect', but I want to know why they laughed at me. Maybe it's because I'm part of no group, and I'm not willing to be. Or because they know David likes me, so they try to make me feel sorry about that. Well, I still have many friends who talked to me. I like them all, and they like me too, not because we're classmates, but we're nice to each other. We are those who want to make good grades. We're not the best, but far better than the rest.

CHAPTER SIXTEEN

I see David almost everyday in the school nowadays. Today we both turned around twice and looked at each other, and I was happy when that happened. At the closing of the day, the worst thing happened, and this one girl ruined my mood. She is bow-legged; she calls her friends to laugh at me because I had a small ribbon in my braids. I felt embarrassed because there were a lot of girls and boys standing by. The fact that she pointed at me is what made me mad. When I reached home, I went straight to look in the mirror, and I put my bag on the bed. What is wrong with me? I took a very careful look, and I saw nothing wrong at all. People tell me I look cute and beautiful. So why were they still making fun of me? It hurts to be among these people and to see them every day in school.

> You know what, they can say all they want,
> They can do all they want,
> But so long as I'm not touched by any of them, I am free.
> I said this to myself.

I felt it must be jealousy. Why else would the girls laugh at me? I'm cute, I have lovely legs and a nice body shape, and I look much better than they do. Most of the students who laugh at me are in Special-Ed classes anyway. Some have crooked legs and all different kinds of unattractive body shapes. I just didn't understand why they are the ones who make fun of others like me. In class today, we had fun and I allowed the students to copy my answers on our exams, and that's how most of them became my friends. I don't ask them to copy from me, but when I see them trying to, I just don't hide my work.

On our way home, the bus was crowded, but Lucy and I got two empty seats. There was a girl who sat two seats behind us. She is in my Spanish class too, and we are like friends. She said hi, and I said the same. The girl sitting next to her thought I was looking at her, so she wanted to start an argument with me. Instead, I turned away. She had lots of thick, dark-eyed pimples on her face, covered with too much makeup, and she looked pale and scary. She asked if I'm a friend to the one I said hi, to, and "yes", the girl replied.

What's her name?

Selom.

"She has a boo boo on the right side of her cheek" she said, and they all laughed.

"They're talking about you" Sel, Lucy whispered.

"I know, they don't look at themselves before they laugh at others". Is that the only thing she could find to tease me? I replied.

"The name Selom is an old lady's name, my grand mom is called Selom", she said again, and they all laughed.

"What you said made no sense, your grandma was once a baby, a young lady and now a grandma," said the other girl, and all the girl did was laugh. It sounded like a shameful laugh too. There was silence, and nothing more about me was said. Lucy turned and she looked at them.

she has very big pimples, Lucy whispered.

She wears a different wig every day to school, In my country, others often think you are old when you wear a wig, and to school? You will see no such thing, I added.

And she's making fun of you?

"Please, it used to bother me when they make fun of me, but not anymore because I see nothing wrong with me," I replied.

The booboo she mentioned is a dark colored skin mark I had on the corner of my lips. I have been told to see a dermatologist but since we don't have medical insurance, I could not get treatment for it. In the summer, it gets very itchy and darker depending on what cream or lotion I put on. In the winter, the skin peels off, and it appears embarrassing. But for once I felt free, I developed a level confidence that I was not bothered much by the students. I walked with my head up and didn't care who talked about me. No one laughed at me anymore, and I liked that. I knew there are many boys in that school that wanted me as a friend, and probably they heard of the many times and guys I have turned down. Even when I saw David surrounded with many girls, I didn't feel any jealousy. I knew I'm the one he loved, and I loved him. I saw him mostly in the library, and it's too bad I didn't have any classes with him this year. At night, the dreams about him never stopped. This time we were in our own home as grown ups. I held a two-year-old boy, and I was playing with him when David came home. He wore a gray sweatshirt he sometimes wore to school. The baby was so happy I woke up with the same happy face.

At school, we run into each other, and I try hard not to look at him. When our eyes met, I took them off. It made no sense that I dreamed so many times about him, yet we didn't talk. I couldn't talk to him, so I tried as much to break that chemistry, but I knew I loved him very much.

> If God should send him a message,
> Do you dream and think of me like I do?
> When I see you, I would like to know.
> If not, please let me know to clear my mind.
> Every day I see you pass by,
> and that alone I love.
> But if I know what you know,
> Perhaps everything must be different.

Sometimes, I felt like I needed to be alone and to talk to someone about David. I needed one who could interpret the meaning of all the dreams. I felt lonely but not alone because he was always with me. I needed to be somewhere so I can sit and talk to someone alone.

CHAPTER SEVENTEEN

In Global class today the teacher was talking to us about first impressions in the school. To give an example of what a bad impression is, he tells of a guest who walks in the school building and sees students in the hallway. The students might not know that they gave the school a bad impression for standing in the hallway when they are supposed to be in class. But what is the point in coming to school and hang out in the hallway? They might as well stay home and hang out outside all day. "They also cut classes and leave the building before the school closes," said one of the students. Another student put up his hand, and when called he said, "because there are no real girls out there, that's why", and Some of us laughed. "This school is full of good-looking bitches", another male student added. None of the girls in the class laughed except the boys.

We had new desks in Spanish class, and since the teacher said we could sit anywhere we wanted, most of those I called friends sat with me because I was good at the subject.

"So you're graduating in June" I said to Rolando.

"If not June, then January of the following year," he replied.

Well, I'm getting out of this school.

for real?

I nodded.

Where to?

New Jersey.

You need only thirty credits to graduate in Jersey.

I had no idea.

There was this girl in the class. She is tall, and I wondered why she wore this short, and tight skirt. Her pen fell, and when she bent her knees to pick it up, her hand covered the back of her skirt, and she laughed. When she got up, she kept on smiling, and all her teeth were out and big. You are no woman! Rolando said. Some of the girls laughed, and people like her with a smart mouth knew just the right response to give back. I wished I had a smart mouth too.

My dad had returned once again, and I went with him to his agent to sign the final papers on the house he had purchased. Are you ready to sign these papers? The agent asked.

Yes.

Let's begin. He handed me one by one until I finished.

Congratulations, you have bought a house.

Thank you. We gave a handshake and then left.

I have been seriously studying. It used to take me a week to finish reading one chapter, but now it takes me forty-five minutes to finish each chapter, and I still wished to read faster than that. I passed my math class for the first marking period, and I wanted to do better than a sixty-five percent. I did my homework, studied for the exams, and participated in class, and still passed with sixty-five percent.

There was a picture collage on the second floor, and my social studies teacher said he saw my picture on it. I hared down the second floor after the bell rang to see my first picture on the wall for Black History month. The picture was a black and white; my face looked close and immense in the shot. The picture was among famous black leaders like Harriet Tubman and Rosa Parks. When I saw my picture, I felt someone who didn't like me displayed it on the wall for the entire school to see it. I felt like ripping it off at once, but I did not. If I had known the picture would be displayed in the hallway for everyone to see, I wouldn't have taken it when my media class teacher asked me to. I felt like everyone talked about it. The most ugly picture I have ever seen!

A picture is worth a thousand words indeed!
People will talk the more.
Some will say it's just a picture,
But I'm afraid of the few who will say,
IT IS UGLY!.

Throughout the week, I could do nothing in class but put my head on the table and pretend that I am reading. I never felt comfortable going back to class, and I wished not to show my face to anyone in the school anymore. Simon, who used to make me laugh, was quiet. I felt alone, and I had no one to talk to. I felt so ashamed of myself; I walked with my head down until I reach ed the front of each class. But, In Art class, one boy tried to make my day.

You, Sel. Where's my folder? He asked.

"I didn't take it," I responded.

When another student walked in the class, he held my neck, and I pressed my head on his hand so he will take it off.

You Sel, the student who asked me for his folder, sat next to me.

"My work looks much, much better than yours," he said.

I turned to him and said, "That is true".

Another student called me to help color his work so I went over and I did.

Chapter Eighteen

Since we have a new Spanish teacher this year, many of the students had quit coming to class, except for my friends. We were taking the midterm exam when Rolando called to put my Scranton sheet up, but the teacher didn't hear him. Another student asked me to give her my essay part of the exam so she can copy. I can't do that, I said to her. The teacher saw me when I turned to her. "If you are seen talking to anyone again, it's a minus five from the two people involved," she said. Rolando and I finished early so we took in our papers and left. While walking down the hall,

During our Chemistry Exam, one student sat far from me, so he called me each time he needed help. The girl who sat next to him listened and wrote down the same answers I gave him every time the teacher turned away. Some of the students called to the teacher's attention so I gave out the answers and after, they copied from each other. When the grades came in, the boy who sat far from me scored 73 percent, and I had 70. "Oh shit, you got a higher grade than she" I heard one students say.

What did you get? Someone asked him.

"73," he said.

What did you get? The girl asked me.

70.

I wasn't happy but didn't want to make a big deal out of it so I took a book and read.

I allowed them to copy from me to help them pass and be friends with.

I have taken out my braids and have a new hair-do that looked like jerry curls. I looked so different some students had turned twice to realize it was me.

In Art class again, this student always bothered me.
What are we doing today? He asked.
"I don't know," is my reply.
Do you think your work is better than mine?
If you say so.
Do you think you're better than me?
"I don't know," I repeated.
Well, I'm better than you, he said.
In what way?
In everything.
Like what?
What do you think you can do that I can't do?
I don't know.
For example, I can stand and urinate.
All the girls around us and some of the boys laughed.
And another thing, he continued, guys can stand by a wall and do the same thing, but you girls can't because you're shy.
With the Jamaican accent, it sounded funny and I shook my head. I also wanted to let him know that in Africa, where I came from, females stand by the wall and urinate too, but I held my thought.
Today I got out of the building late because I had to make a phone call to a lady who bought clothes from my stepmom. The bow-legged girl was on the phone, so I waited. I took few steps away so she wouldn't think I was listening to her conversation. When her friend came along she laughed while they talked. Later they left, and I had my turn to use the phone. There wasn't even a dial tone! Huh, why did she stay on the phone and kept me waiting? Why did she do that? These people are incredible. When I walked away, I run into David and Joseph. I just turned away and hurried out of the building.

Anyway, there is a Mr. Truman talent show going on in the auditorium tonight. During the last period, the classes were half full. They would pay three dollars each to watch body built guys in their underwear. David is a contestant, but I did not wish to attend such event. Lucy told me all about it on the bus. The funny part was, this tall skinny guy looked like he was wearing diapers, but the rest were good! "You should have been there," she said with much excitement. "David was in there, and he got a nice body, girl you should have been there. There's this one guy too; he had all his body greased up, you missed a big thing," she said, and I wished I had been there.

CHAPTER NINETEEN

A letter was handed in class to have lunch with the principal. He knew me by name because I submitted some of my poems for the talent contest. As much as I wished to be there, I didn't want to because of the students who knew me and made fun of me. I wanted my poems read without the mention of my name; this is because I'm afraid of the reaction from the crowd. My sisters and stepmom told me that there are celebrities who attend and watch students perform on such occasions. And if lucky, I could get a publisher for my poems and stories. I have kept all my plans for when we move to New Jersey. Over there I plan to be different. This morning I stood in front of the dresser, and as I looked in the mirror, I put light baby powder on my face, and did not wear makeup anymore. I put Vaseline on my lips and then a lip-gloss. I felt natural and beautiful, but the students do not care about the look but what you wear and how you fit in. I knew I was beautiful and nice to all of them. Although I couldn't wait to leave the school, it's one of the best I have seen so far. The teachers were excellent at their individual subjects. They offered many after school programs including sports, debate teams, religion, and others. They post up writing and other contests outside the school for students to take part. Each semester I had a guidance counselor who assisted in selecting my courses. The principal was amazing, and everyone liked him. He was of average height, slim, and a gentleman. The teachers were excellent, but many of the students' behavior gave the school an awful reputation. The school would have a good reputation if the lazy students would remain in their classrooms and not smoke cigarette and street drugs in the bathrooms. If they could pay attention in class and not distract others, they would be the smartest people. They rather feel they're wiser and better than other students; meanwhile they're dumb. They felt that way because there was an African girl in the school, who had a different accent, who was yet to be Americanized. I wished the school taught more about how the United States became known as 'The Melting Pot'. I hoped someday the studies about immigration will include more countries around the world, and how they all migrated to the United States. I believed if the teachings included how people from other countries also became part of the United States, people like me would not be made fun off among other immigrants.

It's report card day, and I did better like I promised to do. Everybody else also improved, and Lisa got a hundred for Gym, what a genius.

CHAPTER TWENTY

IT was Saturday, and I squat by the tub scrubbing my denim pant with a brush. Even if I had the money to go to the laundry, I would save it for shopping. My stepmom told Quincy and Isaac to move the couches so they could scrub the floor. Lillian took care of the kitchen and Lisa organized our clothes in the closet. Isaac was always lazy, and he frowned while working and Quincy doesn't care. Lillian finished early, so she went to get bread, milk and egg from the supermarket. In the afternoon, the boys were told to go outside and take a walk instead of staying home all day. Outside was hot, and there wasn't much to do so they both preferred to lie down all day and watch television. My stepmom brings clothes from Africa, and we are expected to help by selling them. We are in America, how could we go from door to door to sell African made dresses and skirts? Who does that? The only time anyone knocked on our door was the Jehovah Witness people that come on the weekend. How could we be expected to go door to door to sell? There were African markets to sell to, but my stepmom had a bad experience with getting payments in full when we provided them with clothes, jewelries and oils in the past. This time she said anyone who sold the items would get commission of five dollars on each. That afternoon I took a medium size sports bag, put in about six clothes that cost about $30 to $150 for the big hand woven materials. I needed that money, so I took it to apartment buildings where I knew many Africans lived. It was nerve-wrecking knocking on strangers' doors, and asked if they were interested in buying. Many people turned me down, and others said perhaps next time. I became tired after walking from blocks to blocks. I went into the last apartment building expecting a man I knew would buy something, and even if it was just one item, I would make some money by the end of the day. He used to go to the same college with my aunt, so that's how I got to know him. He was tall, very dark and a big-bellied man. I rang his doorbell but he wasn't home. Outside the building, I sat on one side of the stairs. One man passed by and asked me if I was looking for someone. "No, I'm selling African clothes", I answered. "Open the bag and let me see," he said. I did, and he looked inside. How much are they? Seventy dollars for the one he picked. Could you come next week? "Yes," I nodded. He left, and I took a little more rest on the stairs. This man I've been waiting for appeared eventually. What are you doing here? He asked.

I'm selling.

What are they?

African clothes.

"Open the bag and let me see," he said.

I did, and then he asked me to follow him to his apartment. When we got into his apartment; he offered me a seat and I made myself comfortable. I took out the clothes, and he asked about the prices. "Seventy-five," I said. He tried them on in front of me, and I pretended to play with my scarf so I wouldn't look at him while he tried on one of the cloths called, Bata Kari. Bata Kari is made from hand woven yarn, often sewn into large shirts for men. How does it look? He asked.

"You look nice," I replied.

Are you sure?

Yes, you look good in it.

He looked straight at me and smiled, and I looked at the pictures on the wall.

"Beautiful pictures you have on the wall," I said.

Really?

Yes.

"I'll go to the bathroom and look in the mirror," he said, and when he returned he took an additional set of the Bata Kari.

So how much do I owe you? He asked.

"One hundred fifty dollars", I said.

Hmm, can't you reduce the price?

No sir.

Are you sure?

Yes.

You think I'm rich don't you?

I raised my shoulders and smiled. He laughed and then he sat next to me. I could make you happy, and I want you know that. Do you have a boyfriend?

"No," I replied.

Do you want one?

No.

He offered me the money and held my hand as I reached for it. I took my hand away, counted the money in front of him, and then packed the rest of the stuff into the back. When I was about to live, I thought he was going to open the door, but he locked it. "I have to go now," I said.

I like you, and I want to marry you.

"I'll keep that in mind," I said, and he finally opened the door.

He offered his telephone number; I thanked him and then left as quickly as I could.

My commission was 10 dollars for the two clothes; my total profit was thirty dollars because I increased the prizes to earn more than my stepmom would give. The next day I did the same thing after school, and in total I made fifty dollars within two days. I went shopping with my stepmom and wanted to get cute summer clothes. At my age, I couldn't believe I could not pick up clothes from the store with my money. My stepmom did the picking, but her taste was decent. That evening I bought Chinese food and chocolate cake from the supermarket. I shared the food and cake with everyone and got a dollar ice cream just for me. As for the rest of the money, I saved it for later.

Early the next morning at school I squat on the floor of the locker room's bathroom. I was feeling sleepy and also waiting for Lucy. One girl came in and asked if I was okay. "Yeah, just tired, I said".

"I thought you were throwing up or something," she said.

"I just don't want to go to the gym today," I replied.

"Me too believe me," she said. I got up and headed to the door, and there was Lucy.

Hi,

Hi,

"You're late," I teased.

"No, I'm not," she responded.

When the two of us were walking to class John was heading in the opposite direction and bumped into me with his bag. I turned to look, and he looked at me and smiled away. After school, Lucy waited for me in the hallway so we could walk home together. On the bus, I asked her what she would want to do when she grew up?

"A Lawyer," she said.

You once said you wanted to be an Actress.

I want to Act, Sing and be a Lawyer.

I want to Write, Sing, Act, and make Movies.

I felt like I know what I wanted to do with my life and school was holding me back. Do you know what? She asked, I thought I was the only one who felt that way. I told my mom I want to get a job so I could save for college; she told me to babysit my little sisters and join the Army after I graduate from high school. Lucy lived with her mom and stepdad, her grandmother and two sisters whom she baby seats after school. She also had an older brother who lived in Jamaica.

The next day in chemistry class, the seniors talked about their prom but the teacher also gave us homework and has planned to give us a test the next day.

"Come on Mr. We shouldn't get any test tomorrow," one student said to him.

"Man, we're going to our prom," another one added.

"What's up Mr., I got to stay home all day tomorrow," another student also added.

"Man, I got to stay up all night at the prom," another one also added.

"That's no excuse to be absent from school," the teacher replied, and he asked how many protons, electrons, and neutrons there are.

"We've been studying 'Hydrogen' for the whole week," one boy said.

Damn Mr., one girl said, and we all laughed.

A student kept knocking on the door, and when the teacher went to open it, there was no one. When he returned to the board, Jillian entered.

Did I give you permission to leave the room? He asked.

"Mr., I've got to urinate," the boy replied.

Did you wash your hands?

"You funny, Mr.," he replied.

All right everyone; I will be checking homework 20 to 27 tomorrow.

Damn, Mr., tomorrow is the prom, what you are talking about!

"The prom is at night, and you come to school in the daytime. After that you take your girlfriend and stay all night at the prom," said the teacher.

You funny man, you don't understand, I've got to sleep all day then spent the night with my girl.

Right! Some of the boys supported him.

Anyway, there was this boy that attend the same church as I. Each time I saw him and he is with his friends, he bursts into laughter and they join him. This time it happened on the bus, and I tried not to allow his behavior to disturb me, but each time I turned, they laughed. I decided not to turn until they finally got off the bus. The next day he was on the bus alone, and I was with Lucy. We sat in the back, and so did he. He looked at me a couple of times, I deliberately kicked Lucy with my knee, and we both burst into laughter.

CHAPTER TWENTY ONE

I went to the library during the sixth period because I didn't have a class. The silly boy laughing at me on the bus was in the Library too. The moment he saw me he rubbed his chin and then put his face back on the table as if he was reading. I went to the catalog section pretending I was looking for something. I looked at him, and I noticed he was looking too. One boy came up and said he wants to talk, pointing at the silly boy.

He wants to talk about what? I asked.

He likes you.

Go tell him I said, should talk to someone like him, I must consider myself ugly.

He took a step back and opened his mouth. Are you're too good for him? He asked.

Yes, I am, I replied.

What about me, if I want to talk to you?

It depends on what you think of me.

He smiled; I raised both eyebrows.

I have just had enough of these people with low self-esteem. They feel the need to make me look bad so they can 'fit in' with their friends. I have looked at myself in the mirror so many times I see absolutely nothing ugly about me. I have made many friends, and I can go out with many of them if I want to. I do not feel the need to have such people around me to call friends. I am no longer angry about my picture on the wall, and I put up my hand and answer questions for the class participation grade. I realized that allowing the students to make me feel bad was making me shut myself down. I found the need to see strength in me to be the person I am and be happy with myself.

I received a letter from Young Playwrights one day when I returned home. I am invited to the award ceremony, and I could not wait to attend. The award ceremony will be in a few days, and my stepmom took me to the store to get a nice outfit. I tried my best to engage in essays and poetry contests, hoping I will win and earn money. It was difficult that we could not work, and could not provide little items for ourselves. We did not have the legal permit to work with after three years staying in the Country. Sometimes, I felt like running away, go somewhere far, quit school and find another life to live. But, we thank God always that we have a place to sleep, food to eat, a tuition-free educational system with lunch, and the opportunities to bring out my naturally gifted talents. At the award ceremony, certificates were given out at the entrance before we went to our seats. "Hmm, it has begun already," my stepmom said. It began and ended, and I was disappointed. There were only three cash prizes awarded. The 1st place was for five hundred dollars, 2nd, three hundred, and 3rd, one hundred. Out of two hundred participants, I thought that was cheap. I was so angry, but there's no other way to express it other than to keep to myself. One thing the three winning plays had in common was they all praised America for the vast opportunities they have encountered after their families migrated from other parts of the world. One student told the story of how she came to America during the Vietnam war, how she run from her husband for a brighter future, and how sad it was marrying an older man at a young age. I thought their story was beautiful. Mine was about a little African girl working in her family's yarn factory with her siblings. I thought the judges wanted stories that are different, and mine was. But I didn't get a distinction. I counted on the money badly, and I was utterly disappointed. I thought my play was excellent. I thought it would be good for Broadway if I completed it. I also thought just maybe, my English language was the problem. I knew it will not be difficult to communicate clearly if English were my first language. I decided that I'll continue to write but never will I go to that ceremony for another certificate of Merit again. Should I win, they will have to mail me my award. I didn't care about the money anymore because this is when I needed it. Now I have to find another way of earning income. It took a long time to get a response from Poetry contests so I couldn't count on that. There was an award ceremony to be held at the school too. I told Lucy I don't want to go to the award ceremony because I was nervous. My sister forced me to go so I did. Mina had a distinction in English with three other students, and I had for Art. Somehow I felt like I didn't deserve it because, I took the class for only one semester. I'm sure many others deserved it. Well, maybe I deserved it too. I have spent a year a half in this school and so much has happened that I couldn't imagine what more drama I will encounter in another two years. I have felt like a prisoner, but I have freed myself. Some of the students can be cruel, but I was glad I never quit the school. I continued to write and expressed myself, and that helped me all the time. My grades had risen back up. I realized the person in me was not the lazy kind; she is not a quitter but a competitor. I engaged in extracurricular activities inside and outside of the school. The focus I gave to making my dreams come true gave me the strength I needed to overcome all the pressures I encountered each day in the school. Living among these people in a new country is like living in a whole new world.

Sometimes in our lives when we walk in pain
Sometimes in our lives when we work in vain.
Sometimes in our lives when we walk in shame.
A time will come when I believe I will call Me, me.
In days of bright and blue I have walked.
Day by day I think of what to do and what to become.
But in all I believe a day will come when I'll call Me, me.

The hard times are worse than I thought; our stepmom just called us together, and told us they are going through a divorce. She wouldn't say what was going on in details, but because of that she would live soon. It's a few weeks left for us to take the end of semester Regents exams, and this is happening. I think of my three little brothers, and I wished to be back home with them.

Back in school, I have my hair in straw curls again, and I didn't care anymore if they called me names. I went to the lunchroom, and I saw the Big Bully. He opened the door for me to enter, "thanks," I said. Have you a quarter? He asked. I did, but I said no. I went to the vending machine and didn't get what I wanted. Coming out, there he stood in front of the door with another friend of his. They kept looking at me, and I saw them whisper something to one another until I finally got out. I stopped on the stairs and held all the coins in my hand, and I felt I should have given him. My 'no,' was an immediate and involuntary respond. I didn't think about it before, and I guess the way they have made me feel in the past also made me say no.

Chapter Twenty Two

For the first part of Global Studies Final exams, the questions were written on the board with colored chalks. The teacher referred to the pages in the book so we could look in the textbook. I hated the fact that the teacher wrote in different colored chalks on the board. I was sitting in the back of the class, and all I could see was the first question and nothing else. I asked the teacher to read the next question for me, and he did. Next again, he couldn't read all the questions he said. I understand that, others were also taking the same exam, but I couldn't see. My eyes are big, but I couldn't see well. I opened them as wide as I could, but everything seemed so tense; I couldn't read anything after the first question. I sat there until I couldn't bear it any longer and then tears flowed down my cheeks. I have studied so hard for the exams, I know I can do it but I couldn't see. The teacher announced that we have seventeen minutes remaining to complete the twenty questions on the exams. My pen kept turning between my fingers, I felt so weak, and my heart beat faster than usual. I felt like I have wanted to cry for a long time, but this is a wrong time to let it out. I felt I have already failed the first 25% of the finals, but I loved this subject. He then came to my side and said I should go forward and sit in his chair. I did, and some of the student's complained their view was blocked. One student allowed me to her seat, so she took mine in the back. She had always been nice, and I've always liked her for that. I finished before the seventeen minutes was up, and handed in my paper when we were asked to. I wiped off the tears before turning so no one would see my face. Since then, I carried my eyeglasses in my bag. I don't like to be seen in it because they are big and thick and not from America. The next day, my teacher apologized for what happened during the final exams. It wasn't his fault; it was mine. I was supposed to wear my spectacles all the time, as ugly as they are and in pink color.

I have taken Biology class for the 2nd time, and I felt like I couldn't study any longer for the class. When I studied hard, I failed, so for this exam, I did not. I ran into Lucy as I headed down the stairs when done. Lucy asked me of how the exam went. I don't want to talk about it, I replied.

Are you scared?

No.

She laughed and said, "you didn't even study."

I did.

When?

Last year.

She laughed again.

The night before, I dreamed of David. He stood in a crowd and just smiled at me. In the dream, I stood on the stairs looking at him, smiling back, and then I walked up to him.

What is it? I asked. He said nothing, but kept on smiling.

On our way to School in the morning, he was on the bus with Lucy and I. We did not know he was in the back until we got down.

Lucy how come he never said anything?

You turned him down when he asked you out.

But I told him the reason.

Guys are like that. If you turn them down the first time, they're afraid to tell you something else.

I just want him to say something.

Did you ever say anything to him?

You know I can't do that.

He can't do that either, it's just the way it is.

Since I will be going away, I wish I not to dream of him anymore. I'll meet someone, and that will take my mind off him hopefully. It's about time I violated some of the discipline code. New Jersey will be a perfect place for me to begin a new life.

CHAPTER TWENTY THREE

While we were in the van to New Jersey, everyone was quiet. The roads were clean and quiet. There were no pieces at the roadside to pick up, hmm. Our house was painted, and we unpacked everything nice and neat. The boys went to play basketball at the park. Lillian stayed home watching T.V. while Lisa and I went job-hunting again. What we realized was we were just filling out a whole bunch of application forms all day. I got a job later at a car wash place. We did hand washing, carpet cleaning and conditioning. I was working with a couple of guys, and as we got to know each other, I found out we will all be in the same High school in September. I noticed the attention of one guy I was working with because each time he lifted up his head, his eyes fell right into mine. It was not for once or the third time, and I realized it more and more. One other guy sprayed me with water while rinsing the car, so we ended up spraying everyone, and that was fun. Some people came to wash their car, and they wondered how I could be worked here. The guys made it fun and by the end of the day; I have take home cash. For the rest of the summer, I was privileged to work there. When the semester began, I found myself among a good mixture of students with various ethnicities just as it was when we lived in New York, but the population was smaller. When classes were in session, there were no students in the hallway. In Social Studies class, one male student made a comment that made everyone turned to look at me, but no one laughed. He said, "Africans come to the United States, and they go to school for free." Well, I didn't let that bother me as he did not speak to me directly, nor did he call my name despite I was the only foreign student in the class. Not one student laughed either, but I knew from that day once again that I did not fit in. Neither the teacher nor any of the students made any comment about what he said. I also, never felt comfortable to begin friendship with any of them because I was never sure of how they felt about 'Africans' or me. Besides that, I labeled the boy as being ignorant, in my head, and so I pardoned him. In Gym Class, I came across a Muslim girl, and as she took the interest in getting to know me, we became good friends.

I have responses from the poetry contests I entered months ago. My poem 'English' was chosen to be among the list of winners, and I was happy. The school community also offered a lot of after school curriculum to help those who are talented. I joined the NJ Oratory program for public speaking through the Plainfield Chapters of Mohawk Lodge (The Elks), and each year around Black History month, we would compete against other students from other states. I often felt people could not understand me, but in my senior year I had my moment, coming home with flowers and scholarship for my college tuition after the last public speaking contests. The only thing that saddened me was my parents were not there to see that moment with me. Our Science class teachers also encouraged me to join the American Chemical Society group. In that organization, we are assigned professors and college students to work with in the summer. Then in the winter, we attended conferences to exhibit what we have learned over the summer. I worked in the Laboratory, and learned about genetics and cloning. That was fun practically, but the theory was difficult for me to digest and to present. I also worked on the farm and brought home bags of fruits and vegetables after work. Once a bee in the cornfield stung me, I changed my mind from furthering my education in Agriculture. The best part was that my name went in the book of the 1999 All-American Scholars Directory, Volume 35. I was one of the few students in my school to be a part of the United States Achievement Academy. In this book, there are students from all the States in the country. The one thing I had wished was for the organization to hold an actual ceremony for all the students from all the different states to meet each other. It would contain students like me who have pushed beyond all the limits, all the pressures, and all the bullying. That day when we match the stage to receive this prestigious award, the bullies who tried to break us, discourage us and make us feel like we do not belong, will be ashamed of themselves. When we match that stage, they will see us matching to places where they are yet to belong.

A NORMAL THING

I don't understand.
Maybe it's a normal thing.
You may freely express yourself
But, it's difficult to communicate honestly, what you feel on the inside.
In everything you do, where ever and whenever,
People will like you because of how you look, and how you treat others.
Others will dislike you for the same reason.
Some people are just ignorant,
If you don't fit in their group,
I don't like that, but what can I do about it.
It's a sad feeling, when they don't like you.
Looks like I have no friends,
But, in few months, I will graduate and get out.
After all, it's the last place I want to be.

CHAPTER TWENTY FOUR

All through my life I never experienced what is termed 'Bullying' until I stepped my foot into the high school system. It has been an ugly experience. Each day many other students experience it in many different ways. What clouded my emotion most of the time was loneliness, having the constant feeling of being different and did not fit in at all.

There are three types of bullying, according to the United States Department of health and Human services. Verbal bullying is saying or writing mean things. Verbal bullying includes:

Teasing, Name-calling, Inappropriate sexual comments, Taunting and threatening to cause harm. Social bullying is also sometimes referred to as relational bullying, involves hurting someone's reputation or relationships. Social bullying includes: Leaving someone out on purpose, Telling other children not to be friends with someone, Spreading rumors about someone, and Embarrassing someone in public. Physical bullying involves hurting a person's body or possessions. Physical bullying includes Hitting/kicking/pinching, Spitting, Tripping/pushing, Taking or breaking someone's things, and Making mean or rude hand gestures. Bullying can occur during or after school hours. While most reported bullying happens in the school building, a significant percentage also happens in places like on the playground or the bus. It can also happen traveling to or from school, in the youth's neighborhood, or on the Internet (Stop Bullying.gov). Bullying is everywhere.

According to statistics reported by ABC News, nearly 30 percent of students are bullies or victims of bullying, and 160,000 kids stay home from school every day because of fear of bullying. (Bullying statistics). Many articles and books worldwide also found that at least half of suicides among young people are related to bullying. Bullying is a serious matter, and it can be very damaging to any person physically and psychologically. It is the feeling of being picked on, being made fun off, doubting who you are because 'they' make you feel that way. That feeling is emotionally devastating to a young child or teenager. Sometimes I wished not to return to school any longer, and I tried to change the way I looked so I can look like them so they can stop making fun of me. I could not speak back because 'they' made me weak, too weak and numb. But I found strength in writing down my thoughts about them, and I wrote about all the flaws I saw in them. I found strength in engaging myself in extracurricular activities, I found strength in knowing what dreams I want to achieve when I grew up. I found strength in knowing all the good qualities I have made me a better person than 'they' were. My faith also played a role in my coping toward being bullied. I used to be a church girl on every Sunday so 'they' did not occupy my mind on Sundays. Home life was not the best for me as my parents were not always around and I felt they wouldn't understand even if I had told them. Their absence also gave me the opportunity to express myself the best way I knew how. Being bullied can affect the choices we make about our school life, choices can be positive and choices can be harmful. In either case, I believe it's a good thing to EXPRESS YOURSELF THE BEST WAY YOU KNOW HOW. When you are being bullied, or you know someone is being bullied, reach out if you can and be a friend. None of the girls and boys I called my friends encouraged me to speak about the problem, but they entertained other girly topics that put a light in the darkness for me. Their presence in my life helped me to hang on until I left the school. Being bullied didn't stop even after I left the school because it is everywhere. It stopped because I became stronger as a person, proud to be who I was, and I shone among them as a star.

In 2010, CNN reported that Phoebe Prince ended up hanging herself in her family's apartment, and nine teenagers were charged for her death (Fantz, 2010). The Daily Mail News in UK also reported several students aging from 11years old to 16 years old, committed suicide as the end of being bullied (Tozer, 2005). Bullying is a serious matter, and it is everywhere. You need to buckle up like you do with a seat belt in the car, wheel chair or airplane. You must read more and more about the subject, and the more you read, the more ways you will find to fight it off like a disease. As you read, remember the following tips I have formed just for you.

1. KNOW THAT THERE IS NOTHING WRONG WHOM YOU ARE OR HOW YOU LOOK AND RECOGNIZE THE GOOD QUALITIES/TALENTS YOU HAVE;

Writing short stories, long stories, poems, songs, painting or drawing and that is just to name a few. See such talents as a source of power in you to express the way you feel about the bullies, the people who call you names, who laugh at you and do things to make you look bad. When you express your feelings in a creative way, it is also therapy. If you cannot speak about being bullied, show your writing, songs, poems, and art to someone. When you show it, someone might understand and the door will be open for you to DO SOMETHING about being bullied and about the Bullies. I also used to listen a particular song that replaced my bad emotions, and helped me stayed focused. Loretta Lynn sang that song.

"Someday I'll be strong enough to make that church bells ring
"And when my voice grows steady I can help the choir sing"
(Loretta Lynn Lyrics, 2000-2015).

2. SEE THE FLAWS IN THE PEOPLE BULLYING YOU AND KNOW THAT YOU ARE BETTER THAN THEY.

Think, for instance, do you get better grades than they in class? Are you always in class and they are not? Are you getting the awards at the end of the academic year and they are not? Recognize that these are areas of strengths you have that no one can take away from you, not any BIG BULLY AT ALL. The bullies didn't care if I was smart, but my classmates who recognized asked me to help them with their work. By helping them, they did not join the bullies, and they became a safe net for me whenever I was in class with them, and they also shamed the bullies.

3. ADOPTING THE RAT PERSONALITY

It is difficult to catch a mouse because they sneak to get their jobs done. Be a Rat and write an anonymous letter to your teacher and slip a copy of the letter under your Principal's door. In your letter talk about the behaviors perceived by you as bullying, how it is affecting you and how you feel about not returning to the school. Don't be afraid to use the words or language that will send a clear message that there is a problem. Talk not only about the problem but say how or what you think can be a solution. If you make the letter anonymous, and slip it under the door of every teacher you think can help, including the Principal, you are addressing them to speak to all the students. You are addressing the issue through the voice of another, and you should find strength in that too. If the principal knows you do not feel happy in the school because you are being bullied, he or she may be compelled to heighten awareness of the bullying behaviors. He or she would also provide information about help and support available, and perhaps the consequences for the BIG BULLIES. The next time they would watch their backs before they try to bully another kid. By behaving like the Rat, you are saving many other children from being bullied, you are a hero and no one has to know about it. You can be proud and confident that you have Power over the BIG BAD BULLIES.

You must also know your right to seek the police attention if you perceive any threat or act of violence. You should also include in the Rat's letter you will go to the Police. Do not be afraid to raise such hell for a good cause, and feel good about yourself.

4. SOMETIMES BULLIES USE A LANGUAGES THAT PERHAPS IN YOUR HOME, YOU DO NOT USE OR MAY NOT USE.

In the initial encounter with any bully, you need to defend yourself in the same language as the bully, and if you tell your Mama you defended yourself, she will understand. Your next step after defending yourself is to TWIRL away, to avoid giving any more opportunity for the bully to say another word to you. You can also let them know whatever they say makes little or no sense at all, and again twirl away. Most Bullying begin with verbal attack, and you need to learn to think fast and have a smart mouth. In my experience, the people with smart mouths always have a response in any given situation. I Know I would have one if I was born an American, but I grew up to my mid-thirties before I could develop a smart mouth. If you live in America and don't have that kind of mouth from birth, it is never too late to learn. Your parent may probably try to stop you from having a smart mouth because there is a place and time to use it, and they don't want to be embarrassed. When you are being bullied, it is the place and time to bring out that weapon-Your Smart Mouth.

5. YOU ARE NOT ALONE AND DO NOT CHOOSE TO BE ALONE.

Not every child is privileged to have supportive parents or caregivers in the home to provide adequate meals, let alone spend quality time with their children. Quality times give the opportunity to talk to caregivers about all that are happening at school, schoolwork, boys and girls and all the problems in between. If you find your self-displaced into such a home where there is no quality time, know that it is not the biggest problem in the world. You must have a friend, you must be close to a teacher or two, you can write to the Principal of your school if there is a problem. You can also go to the Principal's office and ask to SPEAK, and they will listen. At least one person will take action to help. Remember, that being bullied is not only your problem, but it is everyone's. Therefore, the more awareness you make of it, at least someone will feel compelled to take action and help you.

6. THE LANGUAGE OF TOUCH OFTEN CONFUSED WITH AN ACT OF VIOLENCE.

For bullying especially in the schools, many children allow bullies to get away with the physical approach such as being touched in an uncomfortable or aggressive manner. The children who are being bullied fear they will get into trouble with the school. Schools often have a zero tolerance for bullying and any uncomfortable or aggressive physical touch among the students. As a result, students are punished or expelled from the school. Many children are afraid to respond to bullying in that manner, and it is not encouraged to respond in that way. Sometimes we need to understand that we all come from different homes and the moral values we grow up with are different. Values differ from one child to the other, from one home to another, from one community to another, from one country and continent to another. In one home, parents ask their children to explain their bad behaviors. In other homes, parents slapped the child for the same bad behavior. In some communities, the cultural and religious practices promote non-violence, but in other communities, the children grow up knowing violence as the normal way of life. It can be difficult for a child who comes from a violent home to hang or befriend another whose home discourages any act of violence. What is the acceptable norm to a person or community is the language they understand, and sometimes, it is the only way that some children learn the best. We all are not the same people, and defending ourselves against bullies sometimes requires speaking another person's language. You can teach them not to behave in the manner they too (the bullies) would not be happy by understanding and speaking their language. In that manner, you are speaking to them in the language they understand best. I went to the park with my five-year-old, and a little boy slapped her on her backside. She turned around and slapped the boy on his face, and they both continued to play until we were ready to leave. There was no cry, and no parents got involved. At her school, the principal called me one time to pick her up from school for slapping the face of another student, who was also her best friend. It turned out that the best friend hit her once, and my daughter gave back multiple times what she received. They both shared and understood the same language, and they remained friends and no longer spoke the language of physical aggressiveness.

Scott Flint, the Author of Waking The Tiger Within: How To Be Safe from Crime advises that if you under-react to bullying, it will continue and nothing will be done to make it stop. Overreact to the threat of a bully, and never give a free pass (Flint, 2014). In one way or the other, warn them instantly in the same language they use. If you cannot speak up, alert someone who can do it for you. That one can be a teacher, the school's Principal, a friend, a Parent, sibling, uncle, Aunt, neighbor, community leader, etc. Also, remember that we are all different people, and out there, is rough and tough, and that may not change. Therefore, you must be strong, be proud of yourself and everything about you. You have unique talents that make you more powerful than the powers of a bully, so embrace yourself, remain focused, feel empowered and buckle up.

COLLECTION OF POEMS

A STEP TO THE WEST

Was a place I once I dreamed to be in America
The one place I could freely dream.
A place where color is clearly defined
Where color is everyday
Color is to human as it is to pictures.
But a dog, or a cat is always a dog, or a cat.
I must have been in the wrong place on earth.
Where I came from,
Color is no application to a human being.
Perhaps,
If humans were made of one face
in height and in weight.
And of the same color
Would that be a better world?
I don't think there could be anything better than the world is today.
But why does it have to be this way?
A step to the West, I considered myself, very lucky.
I am, and I am.
I feel unlimited of opportunities
Education was of no cost
That and many more
I am grateful for.
But the people, I call the Westerners
Are not people, but colors, they classify themselves to be.
From one generation to the next
I wonder when it will end.
For what I know, I am no color
I am an individual
I have a mind, a body, and a soul
I have an identity
It isn't red, white, black or chocolate brown.
I have a name
The definition of myself.

THE SHAPE OF THE WESTERNERS

Oh how much I hate to say it, but they make me.
I guess we don't go through something for no reason
There is always something.
Big heads,
Big noses,
Big eyes,
wide thick lips, eeew.
Big sacks, about to fall.
Big thighs and legs.

In others,
Small heads,
Full chests
Muscled thighs
Short legs
Small neck
Tall or short
Got no hair
A dinosaur is a picture I see.

Which people are these?
Should figure out.

He has a "V" shape.
She has an "S' shape.
It comes in different forms.

He stands straight,
Chest out,
Head up,
Average height,
Big eyes,
Pointed nose,
Small lips attracting kiss,

What do you call that?
I say he is only cute!
If tall with all the above,
Could be cute or handsome.

Without muscles,
Shallow chested,
Count him out.

The shape is straight,
Slim and tall
Consider him a gentleman, or a lazy man.
Have no muscles,
From any look,
Can't you tell?
One lazy dog!

And for the opposite.
Long arms,
long legs,
very tall,
all for good.
Got not the look!
Slim,
Average height or tall,
Long hair,
Short hair,
Beautiful and attractive!

In others.
Average height,
Almost have all the above.
But there is a hidden part to discover!
Crooked legs,
Don't bluff with it girl.

Don't play around,
Thinking you're all that,
Allow them to pass,

And let the beautiful ones brag.
She stands like the letter "K."
With fat thighs,
Moves like a tortoise,
Does no work,
But eat and relax,
Only cares about what to wear tomorrow.
She even puts on a wig to school!
And I mean every other week.
Has big pimples covered with makeup.
And not even of her color!
She wears tights, makes me wonder why.
All that big thighs she wants to show.
Doesn't matter how smart or dumb she is,
she's old and still in High School.
The funny part,
She criticizes others.
How could you say some body's name is an old lady's name
because your Grandma has the same name?
How dumb indeed

People as such.
Make fun of others.
When the beautiful ones do not brag?

HE LOVES ME JUST AS I AM

Ever since I showed up,
With low esteem in April,
My kinky hair was permed.
My heart sprang for my eleventh love.
He loved me any way.

I hated his presence,
I loved him.
I'm always shy around him.
He is a Jamaican.
I'm a Ghanaian,
He loves me just as I am.

His friends are cool,
I have none.
So I walk alone.
He is rich.
I spend two dollars a week.
Yet, he loves me anyway.

I dream,
I miss him.
I see him every day,
And that alone I love.
I hope he feels the same way,
Because I love him too.

He dresses in white when feeling blue.
He loves dim colors as I watch him.
And so do I.
We may be odd,
But he loves me anyway.

It's been a year with us apart.
We do not talk nor call.
But each time we pass, we smile.
At night, I yawn for his love,
I feel he does the same,
Because he gives me the look at school.
I'm about to leave the school,
I know how much I'll miss him.
Since we never talked,
I can't even inform him.
He will discover sooner or later.
If God should send a message,
I love you Steve O.'
just as you love me.

I'M IN LOVE AGAIN

For so long I waited all my life for you.
I have kept myself, like a bird in a nest.
Refusing to fly while days pass by.
I have seen many rushe in,
I have held my breath back.
Because I have the feeling I know the one.
In my room,
I cry for you.
My wings are pulled,
I wouldn't move.
I was waiting for you.
T'was a lot of pain,
I could see with my eyes.
I made a wish, to live without you.
Now I'm about to fly,
You showed up a sudden,
And I'm in love again.

A PICTURE IS WORTH A THOUSAND WORD INDEED

It is true! A picture is worth a thousand words!
Never did I think I would say so.
Here I am with little self-esteem.
Of few friends and poor.
Whomever my heart sprang for.
I cannot go for.
He knows,
He cannot come for.
He knows,
I know,
We know.
On the month of 'Black History.'
It is my first picture anyone would see in the school.
Had I known it will be posted on the second floor,
I would not have taken it.
A picture is worth a thousand words!
e-e-w, she's ugly.
It's just a picture a picture.
She looks cute,
It's only a picture.
Others will laugh when they see me.
Shall I blame my teacher?
Or to be angry at myself?
I went down to look at it and it looked ugly.
It's just a picture,
Doesn't mean I'm ugly.
They may say all they want,

But so long as I am not touched,
I am free.

PATH DISCOVERIES

Born on Saturday morning,
of years ago I was a kid.

Education, I started so early.
I was already smart.

My feet, already green,
I, born jealous free.

Passing crashes, I've been through,
Of young and adolescence fantasies.

I'm still in school and dumb,
I can push up at anytime.

Kindergarten was fun,
Even though I stayed twice,
My teacher, Miss Amina made it fun.

High school is tough,
I go through 'fit in and fit in not'.

I found my love,
so strange I knew he's the one.
We both knew at first sight.

College wasn't easy,
Though we made it seem so.

We're stars of the big time,
We are the extended family of seventeen.

The kids are all talented.
Though not all of them turned out good,

We are happy because we're not starving.
Life for some is easy and blessing
With hope and love we made it.

We're old and live with grandkids,
I'm glad my Stevie never cheated on me.

Any moment from now, we're willing to die.
We've had our times, let them enjoy.

But wait, I'm a sophomore
I have a long way to go,

Hmm. I am smart.

FROM THE COUNTRYSIDE

From the darkness, you brought me tonight.
To the light, I stand before now.
Looking at the stars and moon up high.
I see you and me in this world.

Life in the woods, with no light to see.
On the Greenland, but hand do not reach.
Man has to live in hunger and thirst.
Man has to sweat for grain and lick his sweat.

Morning is always bright, just what we pray for.
Kids wake up with baskets on their heads.
No food to eat until the days' work is done.
At night, grandparent tells stories, and mother's sing for crying babies.

Dawn has arrived, all little ones are asleep.
Teenagers dreaming of their sweethearts.
Grandparents are sleeping, crying babies disturbing.
My father is thinking of the morrow.

But now I have seen the light, I'll show to them all
In their hearts, they'll come from the dark like me.
I stand on this brick, feeling about to fly!
I'll go and fly with them all.

SILENT PEACE

Silent peace I want, of free mind at night to sleep.
Away for months they go, my younger siblings I take care of.
Almost the same age as me, but they say I'm the oldest,
And I don't want to be.

Why at night do we resolve problems?
While they are asleep.
Living me alone,
That makes me cry.
Because I want to sleep too.

I wonder why,
It hurts when not appreciated.
At least not at night,
Cos I want to sleep like the rest.
And wake up free minded.

At night I cry for myself.
I don't want to be the oldest of all,
Besides, they're all taller than me,
I just hate to be called the oldest.

Of all damages, I don't have to pay,
But talk about at night.
The feeling I hate, since I did not commit it.
Yet, I'm supposed to know everything,
Because, I am the oldest.

Oh, silent peace I want at night to sleep.
Not to think of tomorrow.
To wake up feeling fresh and free minded.
I love it at night,
I hate it because I cannot sleep at night.
Oh, of silent peace for sleep,
at night I ask.

TWO YEARS APART

Years apart are filled with seasons of loneliness.
If we're meant to be, his shadow is always with me.
He is mine; I hate to say,
But I know it.

I am miles and miles away,
But I'm not without him.
For once can I be without thinking about him?
Can I sleep without dreaming?
Loneliness is sad for everybody.

It's like a part of me is taken away.
I can see him, but I can't reach out for him.

Even when there's a substitute, there is a shadow I see.
And someday I will leave the substitute behind.
He'll feel used, cheated and unappreciated,

Can I always do the right thing?
Isn't that somewhat torturing?
Will I live with the one I fell in love with?
Or the only one I have always loved?
The only one who taught me, that there is one true love.
Even when two years apart, like four seasons of loneliness,
Miles and miles away, I will do anything to fetch him.
As long as I love him, as long as I feel his presence.
Even when I keep stretching, knowing well I can't reach,
There's always a belief he's mine, go for it,
And I won't let go.

If I can't sit without thinking about him,
I know he loves me, and so do I.
If I can't sleep without dreaming of him,
I know we're meant to be and won't deny it.
Come here boy, you're mine,
And I'm yours.
And no more pretending.

A TRUE DREAM

On a night, I had a dream, a Christmas dream.
Under the green shade, I laid in my back yard,
And covered with the blues of all the day.
Appeared two giant dogs, I'm afraid of.
One black, the other blended white and black.
Hopping toward me.
I was more than scared to scream for help.
I was afraid.
There was no one so near to call for help,
Then few steps away from me they stopped a sudden.
My heart was beating faster and faster,
Then out of the blue,
Out of the dark,
Out from the high blue sky,
Appeared a boy, a baby boy, with chubby cheeks.
He had his arms opened,
The way he came toward me, I wanted to hug him,
I wanted to touch him, just to know what he felt like.
But as I stared at him, he pulled away slowly.
I didn't know why.
One thing so strange, he had two wings on his back.
So white I have seen nothing like it.
His eyes so round,
But how could it be?
He came to save my life.
The dogs just vanished, I didn't know.
When I woke up feeling all good,
For a while and thought about it all,
I felt like I have seen something so special,
I felt I have seen an angel.
He was an Angel.
Yes, I have, I believe.
I have seen, an angel, because he came to rescue me.

EMBARRASSING MOMENTS

Have you thought about times when you feel laughed at?
But come to think about it
It seemed the funniest moments to you.

He was the only shy person in that class,
One time it was so quiet, in fact, we were taking a quiz.
suddenly, there was a sharp, strange sound.
What could it be? Everyone looked around.

But Charlie made no movement what so ever.
Next, the closest person to him pulled her chair to the side.
Another person took his hand to his nose.
The thing has circulated the room,
Gees! It was so strong, no one could breath.

But in all Charlie was giggling.
Did you do it? I asked.
I couldn't help it, he said.

He laid his head on the table, covering his face.
Frankly, that was the last time I saw Charlie in that class.

I came for my breakfast in the school's cafeteria.
I had excess jelly on my plate,
So I took them.

In class as I took off my jacket, its pocket was so big
That one jelly dropped and I picked it up right away.
Making sure no one saw it.
Another one fell out, and this time I'm sure those near me saw it,
It took a while before realizing it myself.
Well one boy attempted to laugh when another one said,
"No speculations please." Whatever that means.

I was so embarrassed, but I pretended nothing had happened.
However, I knew they wanted to laugh,
But they also knew I was always nice to them.
When I finally broke the news to my sister,
She laughed and so did I.

Going back to face that class again,
I didn't care.
But come to think of the incident again,
I laughed and laughed the more.

IF ONLY YOU KNEW

You're just a part of me,
I can't let go.
I wish I could,
But it's so hard.

I try not to think about it,
But I can't help myself.
If only you knew how much I miss you,
You'll fly at once to fetch me
Because I'm alone and broken hearted.

It was like a new light in my life when I met you.
Of all the days, I've been through,
I miss nothing so much but you.
But if only you knew,
You'll run at once to fetch me.

I love you, I love you, I love you.
I can't change that.
Because I do.
But if only you knew,
You'll do anything to let me by you.

FRIENDLY GUYS

Friendly guys, without particular girlfriends.
Hugging every girl and in all corners.

Like Joey, Joey.
Looking all good.
Have girls fall for him wherever he goes.

Friendly guys are pretenders.
They make girls long for them,
And that part I hate.

She's just my friend,
Close friends we are is always what they say.
But when they hug, not an inch of air could pass through.
Pretenders, I call them.

One time he asked me out
And then stood me up.
When he saw me,
He said hi.
Forget you Joey, I said to him.

RICHIE, RICHIE

Richie, Richie
All around,
Everywhere on campus,
And arms around the girls.

Flirting everywhere he goes.
There are girls everywhere he goes.
He's handsome and of average height.
Has big eyes and a long face.
Long legs and arms.
And with muscles,
What more does he need?
He's sure one of a kind
And gets girls of all types.
Do they allow him?
Or he just goes for it.

He seems nice,
He is nice.
To every girl and everywhere.
That I see, I know.
But should he be steady?
For a girl.
Or he should keep on flirting?

Richie, Richie.
Where are you?
When will you stop chasing them all
One thing I like about him,
He criticizes no one of them.
But that's because he likes them all.

Richie, Richie.
I see him every day.
Once he flirted with me,
No, I'm not the everyone kind,
Not all girls are the same.

The years are going by, Richie.
Why don't you give yourself a break?

THE VOICE OF A LITTLE BOY

One time I heard a little boy singing,
Worried about his world and the people.
He said in a song by Loretta Lynn.

"Someday I'll be strong enough to make the church bells ring
And when my voice grows steady I can help the choir sing"
I listened to him three times and, in fact,
It was a note he wrote to God, his mother said.
He wrote it at night, and in fact he was right.
You can do all you want,
If only you have the time
I can sing, paint, act, write and speak three different languages.
If I could do all, I would.
I'll sing in three different languages, and act in English.
I'll write and act in movies.
But then, this field is tough.
Can I do my paintings and dance also,
I don't know.
Because I don't know what tomorrow holds for me.
I see many colors, but only one is my favorite.
Not pink, not black, not white,
It's odd.
I cannot love them all, but I like them all.
I cannot use them all,
Because I don't know how far I'll go in life.
I know I can't do all I wish I could,
But Lord help me, and I'll do my best.

SOMETIMES

Sometimes,
I walk alone,
And think alone,
But no one knows,
I am alone.

Without a friend
A teenager's cry.
If someone should pry,
Lonely are my tears

Sometimes,
I talk alone,
And think alone,
If I call myself a loner,
I am a liar.

Sometimes,
I need someone.
To talk to,
And have fun with,
Just someone,
Like the grass,
That is everywhere.
Only if the grass could talk.

BORN TO BE A MAN

Born in an arid zone
Born at night alone
Was born the man of every woman.

Raised by his mother
A runaway from home and father
But richly blessed by a grandmother
Among all ten siblings or more
And richly grew in every eye,
Where jealousy reigns as the pupil.

But calm was he
As was to be
As born to be, a man.

Like father,
Like son,
Had planted seeds everywhere.

Born to be
As was to be
A man indeed,
Gathered all planted
That scattered and fed.

Gathered all planted
And raised to be one.

Gathered all planted
And raised to be alike.

Even those like mud
In the gutters
On the street
Without a parent

Had been the man
As born to be.
Had been the father
As was to be
The man to be.

More room he had
For more to fill
More meal he had
To care for all.

Free of charge
Under his care
Live the truth,
Enjoy with him.

But a man to be
Such a man he was
Had walked a path,
Had lived a life
Where its meaning
Was to learn to be.

Had shamed the devil
Many a time.
But on his mind,
Was no evil.

Had walked in shadows
All his life
Had found the truth
And kind hearted forgiven.

But still what evil had planted
Within itself remains cold
Until it calms itself.

When good turns evil
As a matter of men
Not satisfied
As a matter of jealousy
And obsession
With the good thought
Of the man to be.

When he
Born to be
As was to be
The man indeed
Again was the hero of all times.
That very old man
Continues to grow
Stronger
And stronger
In my very own eyes.

REFERENCES

Bullying Statistics: Bullying and Suicide.
http://www.bullyingstatistics.org/content/bullying-and-suicide.html

Fantz A., (2010): Is your child being bullied? How to know, cope and make it stop CNN
http://www.cnn.com/2010/HEALTH/03/30/bullying.signs/

Flint, S., (2014): Teaching your Child To Fight Back Against Bullies. An Excerpt
From Waking The Tiger Within. Turtle Press Martial Arts Books and videos.
http://www.turtlepress.com/training/teaching-your-child-to-fight-back-against-bullies

Thomas A. D. & Les W.: Loretta Lynn Lyrics
Copyright: Sure-Fire Music Company, Unichappell Music Inc.
http://www.azlyrics.com/lyrics/lorettalynn/whenihearmychildrenpray.html

TOZER, J.,(2015): Boy 'driven to suicide by bullies'. Daily Mail. Associated
Newspapers Ltd.
http://www.dailymail.co.uk/news/article-187330/Boy-driven-suicide-bullies.html

Stop bullying. U.S. Department of Health & Human Services
www.stopbullying.gov/what-is-bullying/definition/#types

AUTHOR BIOGRAPHY

Ami Dzissah was born in Ghana, West Africa and she migrated to the United states at age 16 in summer of 1996. In May 2003, she graduated from Herbert Lehman College in Bronx of New York with Baccalaureate Degree in Nursing. In May 2012, she graduated with Masters Degree in Nursing Administration from The College of Mount Saint Vincent in New York. She continues to work as a Registered Nurse while dedicating her time to a writing career.

OTHER BOOKS BY THE AUTHOR

THE WESTERNERS

A WORLD OF BEAUTIFUL COLORS

Printed in the United States
By Bookmasters